ALSO BY HAROLD BLOOM

SHAKESPEARE'S PERSONALITIES

IAGO

THE STRATEGIES OF EVIL

HAROLD BLOOM

SCRIBNER

New York   London   Toronto   Sydney   New Delhi

Scribner
An Imprint of Simon & Schuster, Inc.
1230 Avenue of the Americas
New York, NY 10020

First Scribner trade paperback edition October 2019

SCRIBNER and design are registered trademarks of The Gale Group, Inc.,
used under license by Simon & Schuster, Inc., the publisher of this work.

For information about special discounts for bulk purchases,
please contact Simon & Schuster Special Sales at 1-866-506-1949
or business@simonandschuster.com.

The Simon & Schuster Speakers Bureau can bring authors to your live event.
For more information or to book an event, contact the Simon & Schuster Speakers
Bureau at 1-866-248-3049 or visit our website at www.simonspeakers.com.

Interior design by Erich Hobbing

Manufactured in the United States of America

1 3 5 7 9 10 8 6 4 2

Library of Congress Control Number: 2018288711

ISBN 978-1-5011-6422-4
ISBN 978-1-5011-6423-1 (pbk)
ISBN 978-1-5011-6424-8 (ebook)

For David Bromwich

Contents

Acknowledgments

I am happy to thank Nan Graham, my devoted editor, and Alice Kenney, for her kindness and constancy as my research assistant. As always I am indebted to Glen Hartley and Lynn Chu, my literary agents for the last thirty years. To Glen Hartley I have the particular debt that he suggested this sequence of five volumes on Shakespeare's personalities. I am also grateful for the skilled editorial work of Tamar McCollom and Stephanie Evans.

The dedication is to the most gifted student I have ever taught, who goes on teaching me.

Author's Note

I follow David Bevington's text of *Othello*, in the fifth edition of his *The Complete Works of Shakespeare* (2004). Bevington bases his work on the First Folio (1623). I have repunctuated in a few places, in accordance with my understanding of the text. Sometimes I have restored Shakespeare's language where I think traditional emendations are unfortunate.

IAGO

THE STRATEGIES OF EVIL

CHAPTER 1

Keep Up Your Bright Swords, for the Dew Will Rust Them

We do not know whether William Shakespeare was ever out of England. From 1585 to 1589 he is lost to public records and notice. Presumably he was making a start in the London theater but we can only surmise. I remember that when I went to Elsinore (Kronborg Castle in Helsingør, Denmark) and entered the Great Hall, I had a sense that Shakespeare must have seen it. There is a tradition of *Hamlet* performances in the Great Hall that includes John Gielgud, Laurence Olivier, Derek Jacobi, and David Tennant.

Even had Shakespeare gone to the Continent, perhaps with a company of actors, it seems unlikely that he ever saw Venice. Both *Othello, the Moor of Venice* and *The Merchant of Venice* convey the atmosphere of that once powerful city-state, whose decline was highly evident in the Age of Shakespeare.

Othello is the most painful play in all of Shakespeare and in some ways it is elliptical and strangely enigmatic. Othello's race is never explicit. Is the Moor Othello an African black man or is he Berber or Arab? In our time there is a necessity that he must be played as and by a black actor. In the initial production in 1604,

Othello was played by Shakespeare's principal actor Richard Burbage while Iago was played by Robert Armin, who in 1600 had replaced the unruly Will Kemp as the company's clown or fool. We do not know whether Burbage acted in blackface or was portrayed as Arab. A Moor might have been either in 1604, and Shakespeare must have observed the variety of African races when the ambassador of Morocco and his entourage were in London during 1601–2.

The incongruities in *Othello* are fascinating and crucial. Desdemona is probably fourteen or fifteen at the most. Othello is possibly about fifty. He seems to be rather absentminded or shortsighted and frequently asks Iago what is happening. At once a magnificent captain general of a mercenary army and a kind of child-man given to weeping, he defies any easy understanding.

Since Othello clearly is a devout Christian, we wonder whether he was baptized as such or whether he converted. If he was a convert, it was not from Islam but from paganism. That seems to argue he was an African black man descended from a pagan royal family. The Moors of Morocco had submitted to Islam. Most African blacks farther south were pagans. By his own account, Othello came of royal blood and had become a child-warrior. Having known captivity, he had fought his way free and then pursued a long military career until he attained the unquestioned leadership of the armed forces of Venice.

His worship of Desdemona is more aesthetic than lustful. Her wholesome desire for him far exceeds his carnal interest in her. At different times in this book I will address the highly controversial question of whether Desdemona dies a virgin. As I will show, the textual evidence is that neither Othello nor any other man ever brought her to consummation.

I have for nearly three-quarters of a century avidly attended performances of *Othello*. The first was in November 1943 in New York City with Paul Robeson as Othello, José Ferrer as Iago, and Uta Hagen as Desdemona. The director was Margaret Webster, who also powerfully played the part of Emilia.

By far the best Iago I have ever seen was the complex and frightening performance by Frank Finlay, which I saw in London in 1964. Laurence Olivier, acting in blackface, was a very inadequate Othello, acted quite off the stage by Finlay and indeed by the rest of the cast, Maggie Smith as Desdemona, Joyce Redman as Emilia, and Derek Jacobi as Cassio.

In more recent years I have seen several splendid performances of Iago, but none to match Frank Finlay. In different ways Kenneth Branagh, the wonderful Simon Russell Beale, and the comedian Rory Kinnear all augmented my apprehension of Iago, but not even Beale matched Finlay. I should add that not once have I seen an adequate Othello, except perhaps Orson Welles in his film version (1951).

Throughout this book, *Iago: The Strategies of Evil*, I will several times return to Frank Finlay's performance. It possessed a tense fusion between hatred and love for Othello. Iago is the ancient or ensign of the Moor Othello, which means that he is Othello's flag officer who has pledged to die rather than let his general's colors be taken. He has fought Othello's battles and worshipped the Moor as a virtual god. Before the tragedy commences, Iago has sustained a tremendous shock that has unmanned him and devastated his state of being. He has been passed over for promotion to Othello's lieutenant and suffers from what John Milton's Satan, who owes much to Iago, calls "a Sense of Injured Merit."

Satan, in his unfallen form of Lucifer, was second only to God in the heavenly hierarchy. When God, rather belligerently, pronounces that this day he has begotten Christ, his only son, and that "Him who disobeys, Me disobeys," the offended Satan begins his rebellion against God. Iago's progeny begins with Milton's Satan and passes on to such High Romantic heroes as Shelley's Prometheus and Byron's Cain, later manifesting as Nathaniel Hawthorne's Chillingworth, who torments Dimmesdale in *The Scarlet Letter*; Herman Melville's Captain Ahab in *Moby-Dick*, and his Claggart in *Billy Budd*; Thomas Sutpen in William Faulkner's *Absalom, Absalom!*; and the two really horrifying descendants of Iago, the butcher-bird Shrike in Nathanael West's *Miss Lonelyhearts* and Judge Holden in Cormac McCarthy's *Blood Meridian, or the Evening Redness in the West*.

Othello lives by the honor of arms and has chosen Michael Cassio as his lieutenant because he intuits that Iago, though loyal and "honest" (meaning bluff and outspoken), does not know the limits that separate war from peace. He might be a stellar warrior, but he has no skills for peacetimes. Iago is a pyromaniac who wishes to set fire to everything and everyone.

The tragedy opens on a street in Venice, where a dialogue takes place between Iago and Roderigo, who is infatuated with Desdemona and who becomes the gull of Iago:

Roderigo: Tush, never tell me! I take it much unkindly

That thou, Iago, who hast had my purse

As if the strings were thine, shouldst know of this.

Iago: 'Sblood, but you'll not hear me.

If ever I did dream of such a matter,

Abhor me.

Roderigo: Thou told'st me thou didst hold him in thy hate.

Iago: Despise me

If I do not. Three great ones of the city,

In personal suit to make me his lieutenant,

Off-capped to him; and by the faith of man,

I know my price, I am worth no worse a place.

But he, as loving his own pride and purposes,

Evades them with a bombast circumstance

Horribly stuffed with epithets of war,

I can still hear Frank Finlay fiercely intoning Iago's contempt for Othello's overstuffed bombast with its hidden uneasiness.

And in conclusion,

Nonsuits my mediators. For, "Certes," says he,

"I have already chose my officer."

And what was he?

Forsooth, a great arithmetician,

One Michael Cassio, a Florentine,

A fellow almost damned in a fair wife,

That never set a squadron in the field

Nor the division of a battle knows
More than a spinster—unless the bookish theoric,
Wherein the togaed consuls can propose
As masterly as he. Mere prattle, without practice
Is all his soldiership. But he, sir, had th'election;
And I, of whom his eyes had seen the proof
At Rhodes, at Cyprus, and on other grounds
Christened and heathen, must be be-leed and calmed
By debitor and creditor. This counter-caster,
He, in good time, must his lieutenant be,
And I—God bless the mark!—his Moorship's ancient!

act 1, scene 1, lines 1–34

Iago's language here needs some unpacking. "Be-leed and calmed" is to be left without a wind to move the ship along, since "calmed" means "becalmed." The creditor reduces Cassio to a bookkeeper, and a counter-caster is someone who counts up using an abacus. The rhetoric suggests outrage, expressed by Finlay with ironic intensity, including the sarcasm of "his Moorship's."

The vehemence of Iago's initial remarks only intimate the sea change he has suffered. Michael Cassio (who evidently is not married) has no battle experience, unlike Iago, who has fought under Othello's leadership at Rhodes, Cyprus, and other grounds. The passed-over ancient is deflated and becalmed. Iago proceeds to state his new credo:

I follow him to serve my turn upon him.
We cannot all be masters, nor all masters

Cannot be truly followed. You shall mark

Many a duteous and knee-crooking knave

That, doting on his own obsequious bondage,

Wears out his time, much like his master's ass,

For naught but provender, and when he's old, cashiered.

Whip me such honest knaves. Others there are

Who, trimmed in forms and visages of duty,

Keep yet their hearts attending on themselves,

And throwing but shows of service on their lords,

Do well thrive by them, and when they have lined their coats,

Do themselves homage. These fellows have some soul,

And such a one do I profess myself. For, sir,

It is as sure as you are Roderigo,

Were I the Moor, I would not be Iago.

In following him, I follow but myself—

Heaven is my judge, not I for love and duty,

But seeming so for my peculiar end.

For when my outward action doth demonstrate

The native act and figure of my heart

In compliment extern, 'tis not long after

But I will wear my heart upon my sleeve

For daws to peck at. I am not what I am.

act 1, scene 1, lines 44–67

We will see the gradual emergence of Iago's demonic role, but at this stage he gropes for the outward show that will conceal his heart's intentions. Jackdaws, foolish and vicious, are invited to peck at Iago's heart, if like a servant he wears Othello's badge upon his sleeve. The climax is the grand blasphemy: "I am not what I am." This invokes the declaration of Yahweh in Exodus 3:14:

> And God answered Moses, I AM THAT I AM. Also he said, Thus shalt thou say unto the children of Israel, I AM hath sent me unto you.
>
> Geneva Bible

There is also a mocking echo of Saint Paul in 1 Corinthians 15:10:

> But by the grace of God I am that I am: and his grace which is in me, was not in vain: but I labored more abundantly than they all: yet not I, but the grace of God which is with me.
>
> Geneva Bible

In a profound sense Iago no longer is what he was. Yahweh, strictly translated, proclaims "I will be I will be." That is, I will be present wherever and whenever I will to be present. Iago has a wounded sense of being, what might be termed a void of inner presence. His god has rejected him, and he knows no other deity than the god of war. There are hints throughout that his endless prurience ensues from impotence:

> **Iago:** Call up her father,
> Rouse him, make after him, poison his delight,
> Proclaim him in the streets; incense her kinsmen,
> And, though he in a fertile climate dwell,
> Plague him with flies. Though that his joy be joy,

Yet throw such changes of vexation on't
As it may lose some color.
Roderigo: Here is her father's house. I'll call aloud.
Iago: Do, with like timorous accent and dire yell
As when, by night and negligence, the fire
Is spied in populous cities.

act 1, scene 1, lines 66–76

"Timorous" takes the sense here of frightening. Brabantio, whose only child is Desdemona, is infuriated though in no way scared:

Brabantio: What is the reason of this terrible summons?
What is the matter there?
Roderigo: Signor, is all your family within?
Iago: Are your doors locked?
Brabantio: Why? Wherefore ask you this?
Iago: Zounds, sir, you're robbed, for shame, put on your gown!
Your heart is burst; you have lost half your soul.
Even now, now, very now, an old black ram
Is tupping your white ewe. Arise, arise!
Awake the snorting citizens with the bell
Or else the devil will make a grandsire of you.
Arise I say!

act 1, scene 1, lines 84–95

The threefold "arise" summons Brabantio to hear Iago's obscene taunt that the Moor Othello is copulating with the fair Desdemona. Iago, enjoying the moment, wittily turns "senator" into an insult:

> **Brabantio:** What tell'st thou me of robbing? This is Venice;
> My house is not a grange.
> **Roderigo:**   Most grave Brabantio,
> In simple and pure soul I come to you.
> **Iago:** Zounds, sir, you are one of those that will not serve God
>   if the devil bid you. Because we come to do you service
>   and you think we are ruffians, you'll have your daughter
>   covered with a Barbary horse; you'll have your nephews
>   neigh to you; you'll have coursers for cousins, and
>   gennets for germans.
> **Brabantio:** What profane wretch art thou?
> **Iago:** I am one, sir, that comes to tell you your daughter and
>   the Moor are now making the beast with two backs.
> **Brabantio:** Thou art a villain.
> **Iago:**   You are—a senator.
>   act 1, scene 1, lines 108–19

"Barbary," in North Africa, is a link to the Moor Othello. When Iago suggests that the children of Othello and Desdemona, Brabantio's grandchildren, will be horses, he is evoking Venetian fears about intermarriage. And then he further exploits those anxieties with his Rabelaisian vision of Desdemona and Othello joined into a two-backed beast.

In a fierce street scene, Brabantio and an armed band, including Roderigo, confront Othello and his attendants, Iago the foremost:

Iago: It is Brabantio. General, be advised.
He comes to bad intent.

Othello: Holla! Stand there!

Roderigo: Signor, it is the Moor.

Brabantio: Down with him, thief!

They draw on both sides.

Iago: You, Roderigo! Come, sir, I am for you.

Othello: Keep up your bright swords, for the dew will rust
them.

act 1, scene 2, lines 56–60

The authentic grandeur of the unfallen Othello reverberates in that marvelous, monosyllabic line. He commands both groups to keep their swords in scabbards, implicitly warning that otherwise the bright metal will rust on the ground, in the morning dew. Authority rings out, as the fastest sword in Christendom would end them swiftly. Shakespeare enriches the scene because Cassio has arrived first to inform Othello of an impending Turkish attack on Cyprus. Indispensable leader, Othello has been summoned by the senate. Brabantio accompanies his son-in-law to a council now doubly weighted.

There has been a fashion in modern criticism to deprecate Othello. Its originators were F. R. Leavis and T. S. Eliot. Like all fashions, it passed. Yet some of its ill effects have proved lingering. The reader and playgoer should attend to Othello's language, which is dignified, not pompous, yet grandiloquent; proud, not vainglorious, and yet insecure. It is open to the freedom of a nature unspoiled by the sophistication of the Venetians, whom he serves.

When told by Iago that Brabantio intends to divorce Desdemona from her bridegroom, Othello sounds out the glory of his being:

> Let him do his spite.
> My services which I have done the seigniory
> Shall out-tongue his complaints. 'Tis yet to know—
> Which, when I know that boasting is an honor,
> I shall promulgate—I fetch my life and being
> From men of royal siege, and my demerits
> May speak unbonneted to as proud a fortune
> As this that I have reached. For know, Iago,
> But that I love the gentle Desdemona,
> I would not my unhousèd free condition
> Put into circumscription and confine
> For the sea's worth.
>
> act 1, scene 2, lines 17–28

Othello asserts that he is an African prince, descended from men of royal siege or rank. If this is as yet not known, it is because boasting is alien to him, and his distinction (in the older sense of "demerits") speaks. He need not take off his hat, since he is equal to Brabantio. It is both poignant and a touch foreboding that he both affirms his love for Desdemona and yet intimates a nostalgia for the freedom he has lost to the confinement and limits of marriage.

When Brabantio, speaking to the duke and senate, indicts Othello for witchcraft in seducing Desdemona, the Moor is quietly eloquent and calm in his defense:

Most potent, grave, and reverend signors,
My very noble and approved good masters:
That I have ta'en away this old man's daughter,
It is most true; true I have married her.
The very head and front of my offending
Hath this extent, no more. Rude am I in my speech,
And little blessed with the soft phrase of peace;
For since these arms of mine had seven years' pith,
Till now some nine moons wasted, they have used
Their dearest action in the tented field;
And little of this great world can I speak
More than pertains to feats of broils and battle,
And therefore little shall I grace my cause
In speaking for myself. Yet, by your gracious patience,
I will a round unvarnished tale deliver
Of my whole course of love—what drugs, what charms,
What conjuration, and what mighty magic,
For such proceeding I am charged withal,
I won his daughter.

act 1, scene 3, lines 78–96

A soldier since the age of seven, when he was at his first strength,
Othello tells the plain tale of his courtship:

Her father loved me; oft invited me,
Still question'd me the story of my life
From year to year—the battles, sieges, fortunes,

That I have passed.

I ran it through, even from my boyish days

To th' very moment that he bade me tell it,

Wherein I spoke of most disastrous chances,

Of moving accidents by flood and field,

Of hairbreadth 'scapes i'th'imminent deadly breach,

Of being taken by the insolent foe

And sold to slavery, of my redemption thence,

And portance in my traveler's history,

Wherein of antres vast and deserts idle,

Rough quarries, rocks, and hills whose heads touch heaven,

It was my hint to speak—such was my process—

And of the Cannibals that each other eat,

The Anthropophagi, and men whose heads

Do grow beneath their shoulders. These things to hear

Would Desdemona seriously incline;

But still the house affairs would draw her thence,

Which ever as she could with haste dispatch

She'd come again, and with a greedy ear

Devour up my discourse. Which I, observing,

Took once a pliant hour, and found good means

To draw from her a prayer of earnest heart

That I would all my pilgrimage dilate,

Whereof by parcels she had something heard,

But not intentively. I did consent,

And often did beguile her of her tears,

When I did speak of some distressful stroke

That my youth suffered. My story being done,
She gave me for my pains a world of sighs.
She swore, in faith 'twas strange, 'twas passing strange,
'Twas pitiful, 'twas wondrous pitiful.
She wished she had not heard it, yet she wished
That heaven had made her such a man. She thanked me,
And bade me, if I had a friend that loved her,
I should but teach him how to tell my story,
And that would woo her. Upon this hint I spake.
She loved me for the dangers I had passed,
And I loved her that she did pity them.
This only is the witchcraft I have used.

act 1, scene 3, lines 130–71

This marvelous recital wins the heart. The Moor heroically, whether in caverns ("antres") or desolate wastelands, endured captivity and redemption, man-eaters and monstrosities, and survived with renewed vigor. Two wonderfully balanced lines sum up the courtship of Desdemona and Othello:

She loved me for the dangers I had passed,
And I loved her that she did pity them.

This evokes a gracious comment from the duke: "I think this tale would win my daughter too." Desdemona's beautiful affirmation lingers mournfully in a tragedy that ends with Othello's brutal murder of his bride:

That I did love the Moor to live with him,
My downright violence and storm of fortunes
May trumpet to the world. My heart's subdued
Even to the very quality of my lord.
I saw Othello's visage in his mind,
And to his honors and his valiant parts
Did I my soul and fortunes consecrate.

act 1, scene 3, lines 250–56

A bold affirmation, this begins by admitting her breach of societal customs and pays tribute to Othello's authentic qualities of mind and spirit. She pleads to go with him to Cyprus, in order to accomplish their consummation. Seconding her, Othello intimates a curious diffidence in regard to that fulfillment:

Let her have your voice.
Vouch with me, heaven, I therefore beg it not
To please the palate of my appetite,
Nor to comply with heat—the young affects
In me defunct—and proper satisfaction,
But to be free and bounteous to her mind.
And heaven defend your good souls that you think
I will your serious and great business scant
For she is with me. No, when light-wing'd toys
Of feather'd Cupid seel with wanton dullness
My speculative and officed instruments,
That my disports corrupt and taint my business,

Let huswives make a skillet of my helm,
And all indign and base adversities
Make head against my estimation!

act 1, scene 3, lines 262–76

We can wonder how much sexual experience the Moor possesses. It seems unlikely that so long a military career has been devoid of eros, and yet that is uncertain. Freshly married, he shows little urgency for consummation. Shakespeare, as always, is a master of ellipsis. You have to muse on what he has omitted. *Othello, the Moor of Venice* is not Verdi's *Otello*. I myself suspect that Desdemona will die a virgin, though that remains a minority view.

Brabantio, soon to die of grief, allows himself a bitter couplet:

Look to her, Moor, if thou hast eyes to see.
She has deceived her father, and may thee.

Othello's response is uncannily prophetic:

My life upon her faith!—Honest Iago,
My Desdemona must I leave to thee.
I prithee, let thy wife attend on her,
And bring them after in the best advantage.
Come, Desdemona, I have but an hour
Of love, of wordly matters and direction,
To spend with thee. We must obey the time.

act 1, scene 3, lines 294–302

Military instructions and related matters scarcely allow more than a few minutes of love in that hasty hour. To obey the time is to meet the present crisis, and not to embrace Desdemona.

Honest Iago and Roderigo remain onstage as Desdemona and Othello depart. "Honest" has inspired much commentary, particularly of easy irony, and runs like an undersong throughout the play. Overtly it means bluff, hearty, plainspoken, rather than truth-telling. Iago is trenchant in responding to Roderigo's despair:

> O villainous! I have looked upon the world for four
> times seven years, and since I could distinguish betwixt
> a benefit and an injury, I never found man that knew
> how to love himself. Ere I would say I would drown
> myself for the love of a guinea hen, I would change my
> humanity with a baboon.
>
> act 1, scene 3, lines 312–16

Dismissing Roderigo's nonsense, Iago informs us that he has yet to find a man that knows how to love himself. "Love" might as well be the hatred of all others. A guinea hen is a whore, and Iago's humanity hardly matches a baboon's.

Roderigo: What should I do? I confess it is my shame to be so fond, but it is not in my virtue to amend it.
Iago: Virtue? A fig! 'Tis in ourselves that we are thus or thus. Our bodies are our gardens, to the which our wills are gardeners; so that if we will plant nettles or sow lettuce, set hyssop and weed up thyme, supply it with one

gender of herbs or distract it with many, either to have
it sterile with idleness or manured with industry—why,
the power and corrigible authority of this lies in our
wills. If the beam of our lives had not one scale of reason
to poise another of sensuality, the blood and baseness
of our natures would conduct us to most preposterous
conclusions. But we have reason to cool our raging
motions, our carnal stings, our unbitted lusts, whereof I
take this that you call love to be a sect or scion.

act 1, scene 3, lines 316–28

Giving the fig to virtue is to insult it. The will as gardener is
supreme. The balance of life requires reason to outweigh sensuality,
our natural lusts. Love is merely an offshoot of uncontrolled desire.

Roderigo: It cannot be.

Iago: It is merely a lust of the blood and a permission of
the will. Come, be a man. Drown thyself? Drown cats
and blind puppies. I have professed me thy friend,
and I confess me knit to thy deserving with cables of
perdurable toughness. I could never better stead thee
than now. Put money in thy purse. Follow thou the wars;
defeat thy favor with an usurped beard. I say, put money
in thy purse. It cannot be long that Desdemona should
continue her love to the Moor—put money in thy
purse—nor he his to her. It was a violent commencement
in her, and thou shalt see an answerable sequestration—
put but money in thy purse. These Moors are changeable

in their wills—fill thy purse with money. The food that to him now is as luscious as locusts shall be to him shortly as bitter as the coloquintida. She must change for youth; when she is sated with his body, she will find the error of her choice. She must have change, she must. Therefore put money in thy purse. If thou wilt needs damn thyself, do it a more delicate way than drowning. Make all the money thou canst. If sanctimony and a frail vow betwixt an erring barbarian and a super-subtle Venetian be not too hard for my wits and all the tribe of hell, thou shalt enjoy her; therefore make money. A pox of drowning thyself! It is clean out of the way. Seek thou rather to be hanged in compassing thy joy than to be drowned and go without her.

act 1, scene 3, lines 329–49

The bitter refrain "Put money in thy purse" will climax at last in the wretched Roderigo's demise at Iago's will. Desdemona's infatuation, as Iago sees it, commenced violently and will be cut off as hastily. Othello's taste for locust fruit soon will be rewarded with a bitter apple. Desdemona, a supersubtle Venetian, will weary of her erring barbarian, and Iago's skill will complete the estrangement.

Roderigo: Wilt thou be fast to my hopes if I depend on the issue?

Iago: Thou art sure of me. Go, make money. I have told thee often, and I retell thee again and again, I hate the Moor. My cause is hearted; thine hath no less reason. Let us be conjunctive in our revenge against him. If thou canst cuckold him, thou dost thyself a pleasure, me a sport. There are many events in the womb of time which will be delivered. Traverse, go, provide thy money. We will have more of this tomorrow. Adieu.

Iago's hatred is fixed in his heart. If Roderigo cuckolds Othello, it will be a sport and a pastime for Iago and his gull.

Roderigo: Where shall we meet i'th'morning?
Iago: At my lodging.
Roderigo: I'll be with thee betimes.   [*He starts to leave.*]
Iago: Go to, farewell.—Do you hear, Roderigo?
Roderigo: What say you?
Iago: No more of drowning, do you hear?
Roderigo: I am changed.
Iago: Go to, farewell. Put money enough in your purse.
Roderigo: I'll sell all my land.

act 1, scene 3, lines 350–65

Iago's supple and malevolent prose, conveyed with sinuous immediacy by the serpentine Frank Finlay, now yields to his first soliloquy:

Thus do I ever make my fool my purse;
For I mine own gained knowledge should profane
If I would time expend with such a snipe
But for my sport and profit. I hate the Moor;

21

And it is thought abroad that 'twixt my sheets
He's done my office. I know not if't be true;
But I, for mere suspicion in that kind,
Will do as if for surety. He holds me well;
The better shall my purpose work on him.
Cassio's a proper man. Let me see now:
To get his place and to plume up my will
In double knavery—How, how?—Let's see—
After some time, to abuse Othello's ear
That he is too familiar with his wife.
He hath a person and a smooth dispose
To be suspected—framed to make women false.
The Moor is of a free and open nature,
That thinks men honest that but seem to be so,
And will as tenderly be led by the nose
As asses are.
I have't. It is engender'd. Hell and night
Must bring this monstrous birth to the world's light.

act 1, scene 3, lines 366–87

Neither we nor Iago believe that Othello has been the lover of Emilia, Iago's wife. It is merely a pretext for a still inchoate plot. So far, Iago only knows that jealousy of Cassio is a starting point for his net. Accurately, he characterizes Othello as free and open, alien to suspicion. The great cry "I have't" and the triumphant "It is engender'd" are still tentative. Iago will descend into the night of hell to bring back the horrible birth that he contemplates.

CHAPTER 2

If It Were Now to Die, / 'Twere Now to Be Most Happy

My late friend Anthony Hecht, a poet of extraordinary distinction, argued that Othello's insecurity is expressed in a contorted syntax and baroque diction. He believed that Shakespeare's audience would have recognized Othello's speech as ludicrous. In conversation with him, I amiably dissented. Hecht asserted that the audience would have taken offense at Othello's overt Christianity, he being black, and that the Moor's speech was inflated. As for Othello's nobility, it was studied and therefore tainted. Hecht finally relented and granted Othello a painful nobility at the close of the drama.

Othello's mind is hopelessly inferior to Iago's. The Moor's greatness is in his honorable and fearless leadership. Iago discovers his own genius by composing his own play with the lives of others. Shakespeare cunningly weakens Othello's language, in contrast to Iago's supple and persuasive prose and the ancient's verse soliloquies. As the play mounts in horror, Iago's language strengthens, and Othello's crumbles into incoherence.

At a Cyprus seaport the governor Montano and two companions gaze out at the turbulent waters and realize that the Turkish invasion fleet has been dispersed by the storm. Cassio arrives in

one ship, and Iago, accompanied by Desdemona, Emilia, and Roderigo, is next to land. In the exchange of pleasantries, Desdemona
asks Iago how he would praise her. His reply lingers in us:

Oh, gentle lady, do not put me to't,
For I am nothing if not critical.

act 2, scene 1, lines 119–20

Presumably Iago means he is censorious, but the line is dark with
the interplay of "nothing" and "critical." His fear of being nothing
stimulates the critical faculty in him. Othello himself has not been
a precursor for anyone of significance in subsequent imaginative
literature, while Iago has an extraordinary progeny, as we have seen.

Othello's grand arrival in Cyprus is marked as their happiest
moment:

Othello: O my fair warrior!
Desdemona: My dear Othello!
Othello: It gives me wonder great as my content
To see you here before me. O my soul's joy,
If after every tempest come such calms,
May the winds blow till they have wakened death,
And let the laboring bark climb hills of seas
Olympus-high, and duck again as low
As hell's from heaven! If it were now to die,
'Twere now to be most happy, for I fear
My soul hath her content so absolute
That not another comfort like to this

Succeeds in unknown fate.

Desdemona: The heavens forbid

But that our loves and comforts should increase

Even as our days do grow!

Othello: Amen to that, sweet powers!

I cannot speak enough of this content.

It stops me here; it is too much of joy.

And this, and this, the greatest discords be   [*They kiss.*]

That e'er our hearts shall make!

act 2, scene 1, lines 177–95

I find Othello's language here admirable. There is heartbreak in his exultation at this reunion:

> If it were now to die,
> 'Twere now to be most happy.

As they kiss, Iago's aside warns that he will untune their harmony:

Oh, you are well tuned now!

But I'll set down the pegs that make this music,

As honest as I am.

act 2, scene 1, lines 196–98

His strategy to produce discord commences again with his gull Roderigo, whom he informs that Desdemona loves Cassio. When Roderigo expresses skepticism, Iago is pungent:

Roderigo: I cannot believe that in her. She's full of most
blessed condition.

Iago: Blessed fig's end! The wine she drinks is made of grapes.
If she had been blessed, she would never have loved the
Moor. Blessed pudding! Didst thou not see her paddle
with the palm of his hand? Didst not mark that?

Roderigo: Yes, that I did; but that was but courtesy.

Iago: Lechery, by this hand. An index and obscure prologue
to the history of lust and foul thoughts. They met so
near with their lips that their breaths embraced together.
Villainous thoughts, Roderigo! When these mutualities
so marshal the way, hard at hand comes the master and
main exercise, th'incorporate conclusion. Pish! But, sir, be
you ruled by me. I have brought you from Venice. Watch
you tonight; for the command, I'll lay't upon you. Cassio
knows you not. I'll not be far from you. Do you find
some occasion to anger Cassio, either by speaking too
loud, or tainting his discipline, or from what other course
you please, which the time shall more favorably minister.

act 2, scene 1, lines 238–53

Roderigo's death and Cassio's wounded dismissal will follow from this. Iago's next soliloquy manifests an augmented strength in language and an excited movement of thought that will unman Othello.

That Cassio loves her, I do well believe't;
That she loves him, 'tis apt and of great credit.
The Moor, howbeit that I endure him not,

Is of a constant, loving, noble nature,
And I dare think he'll prove to Desdemona
A most dear husband. Now, I do love her too,
Not out of absolute lust—though peradventure
I stand accountant for as great a sin—
But partly led to diet my revenge
For that I do suspect the lusty Moor
Hath leaped into my seat, the thought whereof
Doth—like a poisonous mineral—gnaw my innards;
And nothing can or shall content my soul
Till I am evened with him, wife for wife,
Or failing so, yet that I put the Moor
At least into a jealousy so strong
That judgment cannot cure. Which thing to do,
If this poor trash of Venice, whom I trace
For his quick hunting, stand the putting on,
I'll have our Michael Cassio on the hip,
Abuse him to the Moor in the rank garb—
For I fear Cassio with my nightcap too—
Make the Moor thank me, love me, and reward me
For making him egregiously an ass
And practicing upon his peace and quiet
Even to madness. 'Tis here; but yet confused.
Knavery's plain face is never seen till used.

act 2, scene 1, lines 266–92

Iago, who can dupe everyone else, does not deceive himself.
He knows that he is creating murderous fictions. The absurdity of

Othello and Cassio at work cuckolding Iago with Emilia is a private joke, but one that destroys. Iago is a doctor of the mind who induces insanity. So clear is his intellect that he knows he has not yet gone to the frontier of its limits. His fiction approaches coherence but is as yet confused. Compelling others to act it out will make it plain for its creator.

CHAPTER 3

Make the Net /
That Shall Enmesh Them All

To celebrate both the end of the Turkish threat and his still unconsummated marriage, Othello proclaims six hours of revelry, but
within a reasonable compass. He retires with Desdemona, and
Iago begins to weave his net.

Cassio: Welcome, Iago. We must to the watch.

Iago: Not this hour, Lieutenant; 'tis not yet ten o'th'clock. Our
general cast us thus early for the love of his Desdemona;
who let us not therefore blame. He hath not yet made
wanton the night with her, and she is sport for Jove.

Cassio: She's a most exquisite lady.

Iago: And, I'll warrant her, full of game.

Cassio: Indeed, she's a most fresh and delicate creature.

Iago: What an eye she has! Methinks it sounds a parley to
provocation.

Cassio: An inviting eye, and yet methinks right modest.

Iago: And when she speaks, is it not an alarum to love?

Cassio: She is indeed perfection.

Iago: Well, happiness to their sheets! Come, Lieutenant, I have a stoup of wine, and here without are a brace of Cyprus gallants that would fain have a measure to the health of black Othello.

Cassio: Not tonight, good Iago. I have very poor and unhappy brains for drinking. I could well wish courtesy would invent some other custom of entertainment.

Iago: O, they are our friends; but one cup: I'll drink for you.

Cassio: I have drunk but one cup tonight, and that was craftily qualified too, and behold, what innovation it makes here. I am unfortunate in the infirmity and dare not task my weakness with any more.

Iago: What, man? 'Tis a night of revels. The gallants desire it.

Cassio: Where are they?

Iago: Here at the door. I pray you, call them in.

Cassio: I'll do't, but it dislikes me.

act 2, scene 3, lines 12–37

This is prelude to Cassio's downfall. Iago presides over a drunken party, concluding with Cassio stabbing Montano. We are not told how much time Othello and Desdemona have had for their initiation, but it cannot be much. Othello leaves their wedding bed, arms himself, and arrives with a troop to quell the disturbance:

Othello: What is the matter here?

Montano: Zounds, I bleed still.
I am hurt to th'death. He dies! [*He thrusts at Cassio.*]

Othello: Hold, for your lives!

Iago: Hold ho! Lieutenant—sir—Montano—gentlemen—

Have you forgot all place of sense and duty?
Hold! The General speaks to you. Hold, for shame!
Othello: Why, how now ho! From whence ariseth this?
Are we turned Turks, and to ourselves do that
Which heaven hath forbid the Ottomites?
For Christian shame, put by this barbarous brawl!
He that stirs next to carve for his own rage
Holds his soul light; he dies upon his motion.
Silence that dreadful bell. It frights the isle
From her propriety. What is the matter, masters?
Honest Iago, that looks dead with grieving,
Speak. Who began this? On thy love, I charge thee.
Iago: I do not know. Friends all but now, even now,
In quarter and in terms like bride and groom
Devesting them for bed; and then, but now—
As if some planet had unwitted men—
Swords out, and tilting one at other's breast
In opposition bloody. I cannot speak
Any beginning to this peevish odds;
And would in action glorious I had lost
Those legs that brought me to a part of it!
Othello: How comes it, Michael, you are thus forgot?
Cassio: I pray you, pardon me. I cannot speak.
Othello: Worthy Montano, you were wont be civil;
The gravity and stillness of your youth
The world hath noted, and your name is great
In mouths of wisest censure. What's the matter,
That you unlace your reputation thus

31

And spend your rich opinion for the name
Of a night-brawler? Give me answer to it.
Montano: Worthy Othello, I am hurt to danger.
Your officer, Iago, can inform you—
While I spare speech, which something now offends me—
Of all that I do know; nor know I aught
By me that's said or done amiss this night,
Unless self-charity be sometimes a vice,
And to defend ourselves it be a sin
When violence assails us.

act 2, scene 3, lines 142–82

Iago is both dramatist and skilled actor. He has limned this night scene, and it is one of his best. Cassio, shamed and drunk, is silent. As for Montano, his bewilderment is sincere. We hear the voice of Othello at its most authentic, insisting on the division between the camps of peace and war:

Now, by heaven,
My blood begins my safer guides to rule,
And passion, having my best judgment collied,
Essays to lead the way. Zounds, if I stir,
Or do but lift this arm, the best of you
Shall sink in my rebuke. Give me to know
How this foul rout began, who set it on;
And he that is approved in this offense,
Though he had twinned with me, both at a birth,
Shall lose me. What? In a town of war,

Yet wild, the people's hearts brim full of fear,

To manage private and domestic quarrel?

In night, and on the court and guard of safety?

'Tis monstrous. Iago, who began't?

                                        act 2, scene 3, lines 182–95

His "blood" is his anger and threatens to overcome his reason. Passion for order is darkened ("collied") yet attempts to lead the way into discipline. Power is heard in the threat to cut down anyone who continues the scuffle.

Montano appeals to Iago's professionalism, that the truth be told. Iago's version lies like truth, indicting Cassio while pretending to defend him, and removing him from his rank:

Othello: I know, Iago,

Thy honesty and love doth mince this matter,

Making it light to Cassio. Cassio, I love thee,

But nevermore be officer of mine.

Enter Desdemona, attended.

Look if my gentle love be not raised up.

I'll make thee an example.

Desdemona: What is the matter, dear?

Othello: All's well now, sweeting;

Come away to bed. [*To Montano*] Sir, for your hurts,

Myself will be your surgeon.—Lead him off.

[*Montano is led off.*]

Iago, look with care about the town

And silence those whom this vile brawl distracted.

Come, Desdemona. 'Tis the soldier's life
To have their balmy slumbers waked with strife.
Exit, with all but Iago and Cassio.

act 2, scene 3, lines 224–35

Presumably those slumbers were postcoition, and yet we do not know. Left alone together, Iago weaves Cassio more securely into the net:

Iago: You or any man living may be drunk at a time, man. I'll
tell you what you shall do. Our general's wife is now the
general—I may say so in this respect, for that he hath
devoted and given up himself to the contemplation,
mark, and denotement of her parts and graces. Confess
yourself freely to her; importune her help to put you
in your place again. She is of so free, so kind, so apt,
so blessed a disposition, that she holds it a vice in her
goodness not to do more than she is requested. This
broken joint between you and her husband entreat her to
splinter; and, my fortunes against any lay worth naming,
this crack of your love shall grow stronger than it was
before.
Cassio: You advise me well.
Iago: I protest, in the sincerity of love and honest kindness.
Cassio: I think it freely; and betimes in the morning I will
beseech the virtuous Desdemona to undertake for me. I
am desperate of my fortunes if they check me here.

Iago: You are in the right. Good night, Lieutenant. I must to
    the watch.

Cassio: Good night, honest Iago.   *Exit Cassio.*

                      act 2, scene 3, lines 279–95

Honest Iago, kindled by his own cunning, is inspired to his
most exuberant soliloquy:

And what's he then that says I play the villain,
When this advice is free I give, and honest,
Probal to thinking, and indeed the course
To win the Moor again? For 'tis most easy
Th'inclining Desdemona to subdue
In any honest suit; she's framed as fruitful
As the free elements. And then for her
To win the Moor—were't to renounce his baptism,
All seals and symbols of redeemèd sin,
His soul is so enfettered to her love
That she may make, unmake, do what she list,
Even as her appetite shall play the god
With his weak function. How am I then a villain,
To counsel Cassio to this parallel course
Directly to his good? Divinity of hell!
When devils will the blackest sins put on,
They do suggest at first with heavenly shows,
As I do now. For whiles this honest fool
Plies Desdemona to repair his fortune,

And she for him pleads strongly to the Moor,
I'll pour this pestilence into his ear,
That she repeals him for her body's lust;
And by how much she strives to do him good,
She shall undo her credit with the Moor.
So will I turn her virtue into pitch,
And out of her own goodness make the net
That shall enmesh them all.

act 2, scene 3, lines 296–322

He commends himself as free or generous, probal or reasonable, guileless, and an honest broker. Zest exfoliates into his excited rhythms. The Moor, categorized as sexually puny, is captive to Desdemona's lust. Iago's great invocation "Divinity of hell!" is passionately sincere. His fellow devils, instigating sins, initially tempt with the gestures of heaven. "As I do now" is a fine dramatic touch. Like Claudius poisoning King Hamlet, Iago will pour pestilence into Othello's ear, as the insinuation that Desdemona pleads for Cassio so as to enjoy him lustfully. Pitch, which ensnares, will be the transformation of her virtue. A closing flourish, worthy of Satan, celebrates the net that will be woven out of Desdemona's noble goodness.

Setting up again his gull Roderigo, Iago enlarges his plot:

Two things are to be done.
My wife must move for Cassio to her mistress;
I'll set her on;
Myself the while to draw the Moor apart

And bring him jump when he may Cassio find
Soliciting his wife. Ay, that's the way.
Dull not device by coldness and delay.

act 2, scene 3, lines 340–46

Emilia is to plead Cassio's case to Desdemona, and with precise timing, Iago will bring Othello to behold Cassio imploring her assistance. Zeal must advance the plot.

CHAPTER 4

When I Love Thee Not, / Chaos Is Come Again

It goes as Iago planned. Desdemona petitions Othello for Cassio and receives a gracious reply.

Othello: I will deny thee nothing.
Whereon, I do beseech thee, grant me this,
To leave me but a little to myself.
Desdemona: Shall I deny you? No. Farewell, my lord.
Othello: Farewell, my Desdemona. I'll come to thee straight.
Desdemona: Emilia, come. Be as your fancies teach you;
Whate'er you be, I am obedient.   *Exit with Emilia.*
Othello: Excellent wretch! Perdition catch my soul,
But I do love thee! And when I love thee not,
Chaos is come again.

                                        act 3, scene 3, lines 91–100

The endearing "Excellent wretch!" preludes Othello's fate. When he comes to believe that his love is betrayed, the primal abyss will swallow him. And Iago times the precise opportunity he has prepared:

Iago: My noble lord—

Othello: What dost thou say, Iago?

Iago: Did Michael Cassio, when you wooed my lady,
Know of your love?

Othello: He did, from first to last. Why dost thou ask?

Iago: But for a satisfaction of my thought;
No further harm.

Othello: Why of thy thought, Iago?

Iago: I did not think he had been acquainted with her.

Othello: O yes; and went between us very oft.

Iago: Indeed?

Othello: Indeed? Ay, indeed. Discern'st thou aught in that?
Is he not honest?

Iago: Honest, my lord?

Othello: Honest. Ay, honest.

Iago: My lord, for aught I know.

Othello: What dost thou think?

Iago: Think, my lord?

Othello: "Think, my lord?" By heaven, thou echo'st me,
As if there were some monster in thy thought
Too hideous to be shown. Thou dost mean something.
I heard thee say even now, thou lik'st not that,
When Cassio left my wife. What didst not like?
And when I told thee he was of my counsel
In my whole course of wooing, thou criedst, "Indeed?"
And didst contract and purse thy brow together
As if thou then hadst shut up in thy brain
Some horrible conceit. If thou dost love me,

Show me thy thought.

Iago: My lord, you know I love you.

Othello: I think thou dost;

And, for I know thou art full of love and honesty,

And weigh'st thy words before thou giv'st them breath,

Therefore these stops of thine fright me the more;

For such things in a false disloyal knave

Are tricks of custom, but in a man that's just

They're close dilations, working from the heart

That passion cannot rule.

Iago: For Michael Cassio,

I dare be sworn I think that he is honest.

Othello: I think so too.

Iago: Men should be what they seem;

Or those that be not, would they might seem none!

Othello: Certain men should be what they seem.

Iago: Why then, I think Cassio's an honest man.

act 3, scene 3, lines 101–43

This is masterful. Iago directs Othello, step-by-step, into the borderland of doubt. The pacing is an intricate dance movement, where only the instructor is adept. Like a slow learner, Othello cannot keep up, and his unease augments:

Othello: Nay, yet there's more in this.

I prithee, speak to me as to thy thinkings,

As thou dost ruminate, and give thy worst of thoughts

The worst of words.

Iago: Good my lord, pardon me.

Though I am bound to every act of duty,

I am not bound to that all slaves are free to.

Utter my thoughts? Why, say they are vile and false,

As where's that palace whereinto foul things

Sometimes intrude not? Who has a breast so pure

But some uncleanly apprehensions

Keep leets and law days, and in sessions sit

With meditations lawful?

act 3, scene 3, lines 144–54

Leets are minor courts, and law days are when courts hold session. Even Honest Iago entertains impure thoughts in his heart.

Othello: Thou dost conspire against thy friend, Iago,

If thou but think'st him wronged and mak'st his ear

A stranger to thy thoughts.

Iago: I do beseech you,

Though I perchance am vicious in my guess—

As I confess it is my nature's plague

To spy into abuses, and oft my jealousy

Shapes faults that are not—that your wisdom then,

From one that so imperfectly conceits,

Would take no notice, nor build yourself a trouble

Out of his scattering and unsure observance.

It were not for your quiet nor your good,

Nor for my manhood, honesty, and wisdom,

To let you know my thoughts.

Othello: What dost thou mean?

Iago: Good name in man and woman, dear my lord,

Is the immediate jewel of their souls.

Who steals my purse steals trash; 'tis something, nothing;

'Twas mine, 'tis his, and has been slave to thousands;

But he that filches from me my good name

Robs me of that which not enriches him

And makes me poor indeed.

                               act 3, scene 3, lines 155–74

This has become proverbial; a fearsome irony since it describes Iago's project.

Othello: By heaven, I'll know thy thoughts.

Iago: You cannot, if my heart were in your hand,

Nor shall not, whilst 'tis in my custody.

Othello: Ha?

Iago: Oh, beware, my lord, of jealousy.

It is the green-eyed monster which doth mock

The meat it feeds on. That cuckold lives in bliss

Who, certain of his fate, loves not his wronger;

But, oh, what damnèd minutes tells he o'er

Who dotes, yet doubts; suspects, yet fondly loves!

Othello: Oh, misery!

Iago: Poor and content is rich, and rich enough,

But riches fineless is as poor as winter

To him that ever fears he shall be poor.
Good God, the souls of all my tribe defend
From jealousy!

act 3, scene 3, lines 175–90

Jealousy devours itself and mocks the green-eyed sufferer. Any cuckold is better off knowing, so that at least he casts off a false friend, whether wife or lover. Fineness or boundless wealth attends contentment.

Othello characteristically insists on clarity, and cannot bear a dubious existence:

Why, why is this?
Think'st thou I'd make a life of jealousy,
To follow still the changes of the moon
With fresh suspicions? No! To be once in doubt
Is once to be resolved. Exchange me for a goat
When I shall turn the business of my soul
To such exsufflicate and blown surmises
Matching thy inference. 'Tis not to make me jealous
To say my wife is fair, feeds well, loves company,
Is free of speech, sings, plays, and dances well;
Where virtue is, these are more virtuous.
Nor from mine own weak merits will I draw
The smallest fear or doubt of her revolt,
For she had eyes, and chose me. No, Iago,
I'll see before I doubt; when I doubt, prove;

And on the proof, there is no more but this—
Away at once with love or jealousy.

act 3, scene 3, lines 191–207

The Moor rejects the misery of endlessly imagining suspicions, and resolves to settle the matter. He would choose to be a goat rather than brood on allegations that are "exsufflicate and blown" (inflated and flyblown) and moves us with the noble simplicity of "for she had eyes, and chose me."

Deftly Iago takes his general downward, with the gradualism of a master:

Iago: I am glad of this, for now I shall have reason
To show the love and duty that I bear you
With franker spirit. Therefore, as I am bound,
Receive it from me. I speak not yet of proof.
Look to your wife; observe her well with Cassio.
Wear your eyes thus, not jealous nor secure.
I would not have your free and noble nature,
Out of self-bounty, be abused. Look to't.
I know our country disposition well;
In Venice they do let God see the pranks
They dare not show their husbands; their best conscience
Is not to leave't undone, but keep't unknown.
Othello: Dost thou say so?
Iago: She did deceive her father, marrying you;
And when she seemed to shake and fear your looks,

She lov'd them most.

Othello: And so she did.

Iago: Why, go to, then!

She that, so young, could give out such a seeming,

To seel her father's eyes up close as oak,

He thought 'twas witchcraft! But I am much to blame.

I humbly do beseech you of your pardon

For too much loving you.

Othello: I am bound to thee forever.

Iago: I see this hath a little dashed your spirits.

Othello: Not a jot, not a jot.

Iago: I'faith, I fear it has.

I hope you will consider what is spoke

Comes from my love. But I do see you're moved.

I am to pray you not to strain my speech

To grosser issues nor to larger reach

Than to suspicion.

Othello: I will not.

Iago: Should you do so, my lord,

My speech should fall into such vile success

Which my thoughts aimed not. Cassio's my worthy friend.

My lord, I see you are moved.

Othello: No, not much moved.

I do not think but Desdemona's honest.

Iago: Long live she so! and long live you to think so!

Othello: And yet how nature erring from itself—

act 3, scene 3, lines 206–44

W. H. Auden considered Iago to be the apotheosis of the practical joker. I do not find that helpful. Think of the ancient as a doctor of the mind who seeks not to cure but to afflict. Iago is a grandly negative theologian whose aim is to wound a god and, by degrees, to degrade the divinity to nothing. His nice distinction describing Venetian wives is that their conscience is to show God their betrayals while concealing them from all others.

The art of Iago is comprehensive. One of its effects is to render Othello unknowingly ironic: "I am bound to thee forever." The Moor means "obliged" but the implication is that he and Iago are forever wound up in one fire.

Sadistically Iago twists the hurt: "I see this hath a little dashed your spirits." Othello's "Not a jot, not a jot" persuades no one. Iago is relentless: "My lord, I see you are moved," and again Othello weakly insists, "No, not much moved."

Holding on to a remnant of dignity, the Moor rather tentatively affirms his wife's chastity: "I do not think but Desdemona's honest." He undoes this with "And yet how nature erring from itself—"

Iago is quick to respond:

Iago: Ay, there's the point! As—to be bold with you—
Not to affect many proposèd matches
Of her own clime, complexion, and degree,
Whereto we see in all things nature tends—
Foh! One may smell in such a will most rank,
Foul disproportion, thoughts unnatural.

But pardon me. I do not in position
Distinctly speak of her, though I may fear
Her will, recoiling to her better judgment,
May fall to match you with her country forms
And happily repent.
Othello: Farewell, farewell!
If more thou dost perceive, let me know more.
Set on thy wife to observe. Leave me, Iago.
Iago: [*going*] My lord, I take my leave.
Othello: Why did I marry? This honest creature doubtless
Sees and knows more, much more, than he unfolds.

"Why did I marry?" We are reminded of the Moor's reluctance to yield up his unhoused, free existence. And we are Iago's students. We follow after a cunning analyst devoid of our inhibitions.

Iago: [*returning*] My lord, I would I might entreat Your
     Honor
To scan this thing no farther. Leave it to time.
Although 'tis fit that Cassio have his place—
For, sure, he fills it up with great ability—
Yet, if you please to hold him off awhile,
You shall by that perceive him and his means.
Note if your lady strain his entertainment
With any strong or vehement importunity;
Much will be seen in that. In the meantime,
Let me be thought too busy in my fears—
As worthy cause I have to fear I am—

And hold her free, I do beseech Your Honor.

Othello: Fear not my government.

Iago: I once more take my leave.

act 3, scene 3, lines 245–74

We can marvel again at Iago's prodigious resourcefulness. Boldly he argues plausibly that Desdemona, who had not desired many proposed marriages with Venetians of her own hue and rank, was unnatural. Her sexuality was abnormally intense and craved novelty. It is likely then that she will recoil, and may compare Othello with Venetian standards of younger men, and perhaps repent her choice.

In his return, Iago weaves his net more intricately. He urges Othello to think Desdemona innocent, prompting the Moor to protest his government or control of passion. Left alone, Othello delivers an anguished soliloquy:

This fellow's of exceeding honesty,
And knows all qualities, with a learnèd spirit,
Of human dealings. If I do prove her haggard,
Though that her jesses were my dear heartstrings,
I'd whistle her off and let her down the wind
To prey at fortune. Haply, for I am black
And have not those soft parts of conversation
That chamberers have, or for I am declined
Into the vale of years—yet that's not much—
She's gone. I am abused, and my relief
Must be to loathe her. O curse of marriage,
That we can call these delicate creatures ours

And not their appetites! I had rather be a toad
And live upon the vapor of a dungeon
Than keep a corner in the thing I love
For others' uses. Yet, 'tis the plague of great ones;
Prerogatived are they less than the base.
'Tis destiny unshunnable, like death.
Even then this forkèd plague is fated to us
When we do quicken. Look where she comes.

act 3, scene 3, lines 275–94

Even Iago could not have reduced Othello to this whining condition. His insecurities surge and maim his spirit. He says nothing of his love for Desdemona. Instead Shakespeare resorts to the image of a haggard or trained wild hawk, whose jesses or fastenings, even if they were the Moor's heartstrings, could be loosed downwind and so released forever. He broods on his blackness and his lack of drawing-room graces and on his age. It is startling that he suddenly regards himself as abused or deceived. We wince when he says that loathing her may relieve his hurt pride. Again he curses marriage, with its possibility of cuckoldry. This bad moment culminates in the ugly metaphor of "this forkèd plague," implying both the horns on his cuckolded forehead and even an ironic quickening, in which worms infest our corpses, thus cuckolding us even in death.

Momentarily, Othello seems to rally when Desdemona and Emilia enter:

Othello: If she be false, oh, then heaven mocks itself!
I'll not believe't.

Desdemona: How now, my dear Othello?
Your dinner, and the generous islanders
By you invited do attend your presence.
Othello: I am to blame.
Desdemona: Why do you speak so faintly?
Are you not well?
Othello: I have a pain upon my forehead, here.
Desdemona: Faith, that's with watching. 'Twill away again.
She offers her handkerchief.
Let me but bind it hard, within this hour
It will be well.
Othello: Your napkin is too little:
Let it alone. Come, I'll go in with you.
He puts the handkerchief from him, and it drops.
Desdemona: I am very sorry that you are not well.
Exit with Othello.

act 3, scene 3, lines 295–306

It hurts us that the marvelous Desdemona is so unaware of
entrapment. The forehead pain, almost tiresomely, returns to the
cuckold's horns, and the handkerchief, which will prove to be fatal,
drops even as she will fall to darkness on her bridal bed.

Emilia, unknowingly courting her own murder by Iago, falls
into his net:

Emilia: [*picking up the handkerchief*]
I am glad I have found this napkin.
This was her first remembrance from the Moor.

51

My wayward husband hath a hundred times
Wooed me to steal it, but she so loves the token—
For he conjured her she should ever keep it—
That she reserves it evermore about her
To kiss and talk to. I'll have the work ta'en out,
And give't Iago. What he will do with it
Heaven knows, not I;
I nothing but to please his fantasy.
Enter Iago.

Iago: How now? What do you here alone?

Emilia: Do not you chide. I have a thing for you.

Iago: You have a thing for me? It is a common thing—

Emilia: Hah?

Iago: To have a foolish wife.

Emilia: O, is that all? What will you give me now
For that same handkerchief?

Iago: What handkerchief?

Emilia: What handkerchief?
Why, that the Moor first gave to Desdemona;
That which so often you did bid me steal.

Iago: Hath stolen it from her?

Emilia: No, faith. She let it drop by negligence,
And to th'advantage I, being here, took't up.
Look, here 'tis.

Iago: A good wench! Give it me.

Emilia: What will you do with't, that you have been so earnest
To have me filch it?

Iago: [*snatching it*] Why, what is that to you?

Emilia: If it be not for some purpose of import,
Give't me again. Poor lady, she'll run mad
When she shall lack it.
Iago: Be not acknown on't.

act 3, scene 3, lines 307–36

Calling Iago a wayward or unstable husband, Emilia, who deeply loves Desdemona, decides to compromise by having the work taken out in a duplicate that copies the design. She thus regards herself as pleasing his whim or fantasy. With his usual unsavory bawdiness, Iago calls the thing common, meaning a pudendum open to all comers, and tells his wife to stay out of his business. After he sends her away, he bursts into a brief and powerful soliloquy:

I have use for it. Go, leave me.   *Exit Emilia.*
I will in Cassio's lodging lose this napkin
And let him find it. Trifles light as air
Are to the jealous confirmations strong
As proofs of Holy Writ. This may do something.
The Moor already changes with my poison.
Dangerous conceits are in their natures poisons,
Which at the first are scarce found to distaste,
But with a little act upon the blood
Burn like the mines of sulphur.
Enter Othello.
I did say so.
Look where he comes! Not poppy nor mandragora

53

Nor all the drowsy syrups of the world,
Shall ever medicine thee to that sweet sleep
Which thou owed'st yesterday.

act 3, scene 3, lines 337–49

I prefer the Folio "loose," which adds "release" to "lose." There is fierce gusto in Iago's blasphemy that, to the jealous, trifles are confirmations as persuasive as citations of the Bible. Dangerous ideas work like poisons, initially seeming distasteful but soon enough working upon the system and burning like sulfur. As Othello stumbles in, Iago's triumphalism is energized in "I did say so." What follows marks a new distinction in the literary representation of sexual jealousy. Iago croons, with the relish of an art historian, his delight at the product of his researches:

Not poppy nor mandragora
Nor all the drowsy syrups of the world,
Shall ever medicine thee to that sweet sleep
Which thou owed'st yesterday.

I hear in that the birth of the high-aesthetic sensibility of John Keats and Walter Pater. Neither opium nor the mandragora of the mandrake root ever can restore the sweet sleep that Othello owned just yesterday.

Distraught, the Moor brokenly laments his fallen condition:

Othello: Ha, ha, false to me?
Iago: Why, how now, General? No more of that.

Othello: Avaunt! Begone! Thou hast set me on the rack.
I swear 'tis better to be much abused
Than but to know't a little.
Iago: How now, my lord?
Othello: What sense had I in her stolen hours of lust?
I saw't not, thought it not, it harmed not me.
I slept the next night well, fed well, was free and merry;
I found not Cassio's kisses on her lips.
He that is robbed, not wanting what is stolen,
Let him not know't and he's not robbed at all.
Iago: I am sorry to hear this.
Othello: I had been happy if the general camp,
Pioneers and all, had tasted her sweet body,
So I had nothing known. Oh, now, forever
Farewell the tranquil mind! Farewell content!
Farewell the plumèd troops and the big wars
That makes ambition virtue! Oh, farewell!
Farewell the neighing steed and the shrill trump,
The spirit-stirring drum, th'ear-piercing fife,
The royal banner, and all quality,
Pride, pomp, and circumstance of glorious war!
And, O you mortal engines, whose rude throats
Th'immortal Jove's dread clamors counterfeit,
Farewell! Othello's occupation's gone.

act 3, scene 3, lines 350–74

The enigma again is the Moor's fragility. How much sympathy can he evoke when prestige and not love is his concern? Infected by

Iago, he has become rancid. All that matters are his feelings and his fear of lost renown. Six "farewells" are the refrain in his lament for the big wars and their music: neighing steed, shrill trumpet, drum, fife, the banner of his honor, and what he lovingly calls "Pride, pomp, and circumstance of glorious war!" Edward Elgar's *Pomp and Circumstance Marches*, while stirring enough, fall short of the *Othello* music. Even artillery joins the celebration, counterfeiting Jove's thunder. The dying fall is: "Othello's occupation's gone."

The thrust and parry between the Moor and Iago bruise the limits of Shakespearean invention:

Iago: Is't possible, my lord?
Othello: Villain, be sure thou prove my love a whore!
Be sure of it. Give me the ocular proof,
Or, by the worth of mine eternal soul,
Thou hadst been better have been born a dog
Than answer my waked wrath.
Iago: Is't come to this?
Othello: Make me to see't; or at the least, so prove it
That the probation bear no hinge nor loop
To hang a doubt on, or woe upon thy life!

Iago, until now, did not realize that it would be his life or Desdemona's. The burden of probation or proof is his.

Iago: My noble lord—
Othello: If thou dost slander her and torture me,
Never pray more; abandon all remorse;

On horror's head horrors accumulate;
Do deeds to make heaven weep, all earth amazed;
For nothing canst thou to damnation add
Greater than that.

If Iago cannot make his case, his hope for salvation will abandon him, as Othello is a vengeful Christian. Horror upon horror will pile up until all the earth yields to it.

Iago: O grace! O heaven forgive me!
Are you a man? Have you a soul or sense?
God b'wi'you; take mine office. O wretched fool!
That liv'st to make thine honesty a vice!
O monstrous world! Take note, take note, O world,
To be direct and honest is not safe.
I thank you for this profit, and from hence
I'll love no friend, sith love breeds such offence.
Othello: Nay, stay. Thou shouldst be honest.
Iago: I should be wise, for honesty's a fool
And loses that it works for.
Othello: By the world,
I think my wife be honest and think she is not;
I think that thou art just and think thou art not.
I'll have some proof. Her name, that was as fresh
As Dian's visage, is now begrimed and black
As mine own face. If there be cords, or knives,
Poison, or fire, or suffocating streams,
I'll not endure it. Would I were satisfied!

Desdemona's countenance and reputation, once as fresh as Diana's, patroness of the moon and chastity, have become as black as the Moor's.

> **Iago:** I see, sir, you are eaten up with passion.
> I do repent me that I put it to you.
> You would be satisfied?
> **Othello:**   Would? Nay, and I will.
> **Iago:** And may; but how? How satisfied, my lord?
> Would you, the supervisor, grossly gape on?
> Behold her topped?
> **Othello:** Death and damnation! Oh!

Iago, recovering his stride, wounds the Moor with the disgrace of being a voyeur. I think of Faulkner's Popeye, in *Sanctuary*, slobbering as he beholds Red topping Temple Drake.

> It were a tedious difficulty, I think,
> To bring them to that prospect. Damn them then,
> If ever mortal eyes do see them bolster
> More than their own. What then? How then?
> What shall I say? Where's satisfaction?
> It is impossible you should see this,
> Were they as prime as goats, as hot as monkeys,
> As salt as wolves in pride, and fools as gross
> As ignorance made drunk. But yet I say,
> If imputation and strong circumstances

Which lead directly to the door of truth
Will give you satisfaction, you might have't.

act 3, scene 3, lines 375–425

Goats and monkeys are Iago's talismans. Innuendo and inference suffice for satisfaction. In his desperation, Othello resorts to pleading:

Othello: Give me a living reason she's disloyal.
Iago: I do not like the office.
But, sith I am entered in this cause so far,
Pricked to't by foolish honesty and love,
I will go on. I lay with Cassio lately,
And being troubled with a raging tooth
I could not sleep. There are a kind of men
So loose of soul that in their sleeps will mutter
Their affairs. One of this kind is Cassio.
In sleep I heard him say, "Sweet Desdemona,
Let us be wary, let us hide our loves!"
And then, sir, would he grip and wring my hand,
Cry, "O sweet creature!," then kiss me hard,
As if he plucked up kisses by the roots
That grew upon my lips; then laid his leg
Over my thigh, and sighed, and kissed, and then
Cried, "Cursèd fate that gave thee to the Moor!"
Othello: Oh, monstrous! Monstrous!
Iago: Nay, this was but his dream.

Othello: But this denoted a foregone conclusion.
'Tis a shrewd doubt, though it be but a dream.
Iago: And this may help to thicken other proofs
That do demonstrate thinly.
Othello: I'll tear her all to pieces.

                              act 3, scene 3, lines 426–47

Outright lying betrays Iago's own fear and desperation. His absurd tale could fool only a maniac. The fabric of Othello gives way in his dreadful "I'll tear her all to pieces." And Iago springs to his opportunity:

Iago: Nay, but be wise. Yet we see nothing done;
She may be honest yet. Tell me but this:
Have you not sometimes seen a handkerchief
Spotted with strawberries in your wife's hand?
Othello: I gave her such a one. 'Twas my first gift.
Iago: I know not that; but such a handkerchief—
I am sure it was your wife's—did I today
See Cassio wipe his beard with.
Othello: If it be that—
Iago: If it be that, or any that was hers,
It speaks against her with the other proofs.
Othello: O that the slave had forty thousand lives!
One is too poor, too weak for my revenge.
Now do I see 'tis true. Look here, Iago,
All my fond love thus do I blow to heaven.
'Tis gone.

Arise, black vengeance, from the hollow hell!

Yield up, O love, thy crown and hearted throne

To tyrannous hate! Swell, bosom, with thy freight,

For 'tis of aspics' tongues!

Iago: Yet be content.

Othello: O! blood, blood, blood!

act 3, scene 3, lines 448–68

Absolute collapse ends Othello as we have known him. An ugliness surpassing our worst expectations sweeps him to "black vengeance." Iago, in total control, becomes the stage manager of a black mass:

Iago: Patience, I say. Your mind perhaps may change.

Othello: Never, Iago. Like to the Pontic Sea,

Whose icy current and compulsive course

Ne'er feels retiring ebb, but keeps due on

To the Propontic and the Hellespont,

Even so my bloody thoughts, with violent pace

Shall ne'er look back, ne'er ebb to humble love,

Till that a capable and wide revenge

Swallow them up. Now, by yond marble heaven,

[*Kneeling*] In the due reverence of a sacred vow

I here engage my words.

act 3, scene 3, lines 469–79

A parody of the Moor's great voice gives us the propulsion of his sadistic mania. His bloody thoughts flow with the icy current and will never ebb, until his revenge is accomplished. He appeals to a marble heaven that disregards human pain. When he kneels, he is no longer a Christian or even sane. And Iago, in his magnificent genius, urges Othello not to rise, and kneels facing him:

Iago: Do not rise yet.

[*He kneels.*] Witness, you ever-burning lights above,

You elements that clip us round about,

Witness that here Iago doth give up

The execution of his wit, hands, heart,

To wronged Othello's service. Let him command,

And to obey shall be in me remorse,

What bloody business ever.   [*They rise.*]

Othello: I greet thy love,

Not with vain thanks, but with acceptance bounteous,

And will upon the instant put thee to't.

Within these three days let me hear thee say

That Cassio's not alive.

Iago: My friend is dead;

'Tis done at your request. But let her live.

Othello: Damn her, lewd minx! Oh, damn her, damn her!

Come, go with me apart. I will withdraw.

To furnish me with some swift means of death

For the fair devil. Now art thou my lieutenant.

Iago: I am your own forever.

Exeunt.

                              act 3, scene 3, lines 480–99

Iago, happy enough to kill Cassio, still entreats for Desdemona's life. Why? We cannot know. It does not matter since Othello, after giving Cassio to Iago, takes upon himself the murder of Desdemona.

It is no less than stunning when we hear the interplay between "Now art thou my lieutenant" and "I am your own forever." Iago is no longer to suffer from a sense of injured merit, and indeed has become Othello's daemon or genius.

CHAPTER 5

There's Magic
in the Web of It

Two webs, Iago's and the handkerchief's, are intricately worked together as Othello, Desdemona, Cassio, and Emilia plummet downward to darkness. Shakespeare stretches out the agony from scene to scene. We listen, with tempestuous trepidation, as Desdemona manifests her generous innocence:

> **Desdemona:** Where should I lose that handkerchief, Emilia?
> **Emilia:** I know not, madam.
> **Desdemona:** Believe me, I had rather have lost my purse
> Full of crusadoes; and but my noble Moor
> Is true of mind and made of no such baseness
> As jealous creatures are, it were enough
> To put him to ill thinking.
> **Emilia:** Is he not jealous?
> **Desdemona:** Who, he? I think the sun where he was born
> Drew all such humors from him.
> **Emilia:** Look where he comes.
> *Enter Othello.*
>
> act 3, scene 4, lines 17–25

To Desdemona, Othello's temperament is immune to jealousy. But that was the Moor before his fall. The magic of Iago's web trumps all:

> **Desdemona:** I will not leave him now till Cassio
> Be called to him.—How is't with you, my lord?
> **Othello:** Well, my good lady. [*Aside.*] O, hardness to
>   dissemble!—
> How do you, Desdemona?
> **Desdemona:**   Well, my good lord.
> **Othello:** Give me your hand. This hand is moist, my lady.
> **Desdemona:** It yet hath felt no age nor known no sorrow.
> **Othello:** This argues fruitfulness and liberal heart;
> Hot, hot, and moist. This hand of yours requires
> A sequester from liberty, fasting and prayer,
> Much castigation, exercise devout;
> For here's a young and sweating devil here
> That commonly rebels. 'Tis a good hand,
> A frank one.
> **Desdemona:** You may indeed say so,
> For 'twas that hand that gave away my heart.
> **Othello:** A liberal hand. The hearts of old gave hands,
> But our new heraldry is hands, not hearts.
> **Desdemona:** I cannot speak of this. Come now, your promise.
>
>   act 3, scene 4, lines 26–42

Holding her hand, the scattered Moor judges that it shows amorousness and sexual freedom. Bitterly he terms it a good

66

hand, open to eros. In her Eve-like generosity, she moves us: "For 'twas that hand that gave away my heart." Othello alas is no longer Adam. He has devoured Iago's fruit of discord and severs hands from hearts.

Othello: What promise, chuck?

Desdemona: I have sent to bid Cassio come speak with you.

Othello: I have a salt and sorry rheum offends me;
Lend me thy handkerchief.

Desdemona: Here, my lord.   [*She offers a handkerchief.*]

Othello: That which I gave you.

Desdemona: I have it not about me.

Othello: Not?

Desdemona: No, faith, my lord.

Othello: That's a fault. That handkerchief
Did an Egyptian to my mother give.
She was a charmer, and could almost read
The thoughts of people. She told her, while she kept it
'Twould make her amiable and subdue my father
Entirely to her love, but if she lost it
Or made a gift of it, my father's eye
Should hold her loathèd, and his spirits should hunt
After new fancies. She, dying, gave it me,
And bid me, when my fate would have me wived,
To give it her. I did so; and take heed on't;
Make it a darling like your precious eye.
To lose't or give't away were such perdition
As nothing else could match.

Desdemona: Is't possible?

Othello: 'Tis true; there's magic in the web of it.

A sibyl, that had numbered in the world

The sun to course two hundred compasses,

In her prophetic fury sewed the work;

The worms were hallowed that did breed the silk,

And it was dy'd in mummy which the skillful

Conserved of maidens' hearts.

                      act 3, scene 4, lines 43–71

The Egyptian sorceress wove two centuries of magic into the fabric, in a fury of inspiration. The silkworms were sacred, and the handkerchief was colored by a liquid drained from mummies and concocted from the hearts of virgins.

Desdemona: I'faith! Is't true?

Othello: Most veritable, therefore, look to't well.

Desdemona: Then would to God that I had never seen't!

Othello: Ha? Wherefore?

Desdemona: Why do you speak so startingly and rash?

Othello: Is't lost? Is't gone? Speak, is't out o'th'way?

Desdemona: Heaven bless us!

Othello: Say you?

Desdemona: It is not lost; but what an if it were?

Othello: How?

Desdemona: I say, it is not lost.

Othello: Fetch't, let me see't!

Desdemona: Why, so I can, sir, but I will not now.

This is a trick to put me from my suit.

Pray you, let Cassio be received again.

Othello: Fetch me the handkerchief. My mind misgives.

Desdemona: Come, come,

You'll never meet a more sufficient man.

Othello: The handkerchief!

Desdemona: I pray, talk me of Cassio.

Othello: The handkerchief!

Desdemona: A man that all his time

Hath founded his good fortunes on your love,

Shared dangers with you—

Othello: The handkerchief!

Desdemona: I'faith, you are to blame.

Othello: Zounds!   *Exit Othello.*

Emilia: Is not this man jealous?

Desdemona: I ne'er saw this before.

Sure, there's some wonder in this handkerchief.

I am most unhappy in the loss of it.

Emilia: 'Tis not a year or two shows us a man.

They are all but stomachs, and we all but food;

They eat us hungerly, and when they are full

They belch us.

                              act 3, scene 4, lines 71–102

"The handkerchief!" beats like a refrain and prompts Emilia to an apt reflection. We hear in it her relation to Iago and her own gathering fate. It fascinates me, comparing the Quarto with the Folio, that Shakespeare revised and augmented Emilia's role and aspects of Desdemona's and Cassio's but added nothing to Iago's, whom he got precisely from the start. Emilia, with accurate bitterness, remarks that it takes a while for a wife to know a husband. What she will learn is that husbands are nothing but stomachs, hungry in their lust, and when replete they belch forth the leftovers.

The image is prevalent in Shakespeare. Antony, furious with Cleopatra, dismisses her as remnants abandoned by prior lovers:

> I found you as a morsel, cold upon
> Dead Caesar's trencher—nay, you were a fragment
> Of Gnaeus Pompey's—
> > *Antony and Cleopatra*, act 3, scene 13, lines 121–23

Troilus, addressing Ulysses, rather nastily characterizes Cressida's yielding to Diomedes:

> The fractions of her faith, orts of her love,
> The fragments, scraps, the bits and greasy relics
> Of her o'er-eaten faith, are given to Diomed.
> > *Troilus and Cressida*, act 5, scene 2

Even in my eighty-eighth year, I grimace at these gustatory tropes. Male vernacular features them still. Emilia fights back. Her courage will cost her life itself, but in the dark drama of *Othello*, hers is the only countervailing force against Iago.

CHAPTER 6

I Will Chop Her into Messes. Cuckold Me!

If you have lost your faith in the war god, you yet retain profound interest in his degradation. Milton's Satan, Iago's son, hates Milton's God and seeks some way to grieve him. War in heaven has been fought and lost. In Iago's mode, Satan resolves to prey upon innocence. Eve and Adam become Desdemona on a cosmic scale.

Iago, entering with Cassio, is clinically aroused when told that the Moor is angry:

Desdemona: Alas! thrice-gentle Cassio,
My advocation is not now in tune.
My lord is not my lord; nor should I know him,
Were he in favor as in humor altered.
So help me every spirit sanctified
As I have spoken for you all my best
And stood within the blank of his displeasure
For my free speech! You must awhile be patient.
What I can do, I will, and more I will
Than for myself I dare. Let that suffice you.

Iago: Is my lord angry?
Emilia: He went hence but now,
And certainly in strange unquietness.
Iago: Can he be angry? I have seen the cannon
When it hath blown his ranks into the air,
And like the devil from his very arm
Puffed his own brother—and is he angry?
Something of moment then. I will go meet him;
There's matter in't indeed, if he be angry.
Desdemona: I prithee do so.
Exit Iago.

          act 3, scene 4, lines 118–36

Thrice we hear "angry." Iago recalls the Moor's serenity under fire and loss. Anger is new. Aesthete of jealousy, Iago eagerly seeks Othello. Desdemona and Emilia, in Cassio's presence, exchange what wisdom they can on the theme of male jealousy:

Desdemona: Something, sure, of state,
Either from Venice, or some unhatched practice
Made demonstrable here in Cyprus to him,
Hath puddled his clear spirit; and in such cases
Men's natures wrangle with inferior things,
Though great ones are their object. 'Tis even so;
For let our finger ache, and it indues
Our other, healthful members even to a sense
Of pain. Nay, we must think men are not gods,
Nor of them look for such observancy

As fits the bridal. Beshrew me much, Emilia,
I was, unhandsome warrior as I am,
Arraigning his unkindness with my soul;
But now I find I had suborned the witness,
And he's indicted falsely.

Emilia: Pray heaven it be
State matters, as you think, and no conception
Nor no jealous toy concerning you.

Desdemona: Alas the day! I never gave him cause.

Emilia: But jealous souls will not be answered so;
They are not ever jealous for the cause,
But jealous for they're jealous. It is a monster
Begot upon itself, born on itself.

Desdemona: Heaven keep the monster from Othello's mind!

Emilia: Lady, amen.

Desdemona: I will go seek him. Cassio, walk hereabout.
If I do find him fit, I'll move your suit
And seek to effect it to my uttermost.

Cassio: I humbly thank Your Ladyship.

act 3, scene 4, lines 136–63

Desdemona, lucid and yearning for happiness, is conscious of the shadow falling upon her. Emilia, who has experienced Iago, is wiser and darker. Cassio, transparently loyal to Othello, approaches a kind of pathos that augers ill for all.

Shakespeare allows us a momentary stay from tension by introducing Bianca, a Venetian courtesan in thrall to Cassio. Their dialogue nevertheless turns upon the fatal handkerchief:

Bianca: Save you, friend Cassio!

Cassio: What make you from home?

How is't with you, my most fair Bianca?

I'faith, sweet love, I was coming to your house.

Bianca: And I was going to your lodging, Cassio.

What, keep a week away? Seven days and nights?

Eightscore-eight hours? And lovers' absent hours

More tedious than the dial eightscore times?

O weary reck'ning!

Cassio: Pardon me, Bianca.

I have this while with leaden thoughts been pressed;

But I shall in a more continuate time,

Strike off this score of absence. Sweet Bianca,

[*Giving her Desdemona's handkerchief*]

Take me this work out.

act 3, scene 4, lines 164–75

Cassio is asking Bianca to copy the embroidery, yet there are multiple meanings to "Take me this work out." The work is Iago's net, and nothing will take Cassio and Desdemona out of it.

Bianca: Oh, Cassio, whence came this?

This is some token from a newer friend.

To the felt absence now I feel a cause.

Is't come to this? Well, well.

Cassio: Go to, woman!

Throw your vile guesses in the devil's teeth,

From whence you have them. You are jealous now

That this is from some mistress, some remembrance.

No, by my faith, Bianca.

Bianca: Why, whose is it?

Cassio: I know not, neither. I found it in my chamber.

I like the work well. Ere it be demanded—

As like enough it will—I would have it copied.

Take it, and do't, and leave me for this time.

Bianca: Leave you? Wherefore?

Cassio: I do attend here on the General,

And think it no addition, nor my wish,

To have him see me womaned.

Bianca: Why, I pray you?

Cassio: Not that I love you not.

Bianca: But that you do not love me.

I pray you, bring me on the way a little,

And say if I shall see you soon at night.

Cassio: 'Tis but a little way that I can bring you,

For I attend here; but I'll see you soon.

Bianca: 'Tis very good. I must be circumstanced.

act 3, scene 4, lines 175–98

The spirit is light and dallying, but "jealousy" has intruded. I always want to hold on to this interlude, because everything to come is harrowing. Othello's collapse is total, under the careful guidance of Iago:

Iago: Will you think so?

Othello: Think so, Iago?

Iago: What,
To kiss in private?
Othello: An unauthorized kiss!
Iago: Or to be naked with her friend in bed
An hour or more, not meaning any harm?
Othello: Naked in bed, Iago, and not mean harm?
It is hypocrisy against the devil.
They that mean virtuously and yet do so,
The devil their virtue tempts, and they tempt heaven.
Iago: If they do nothing, 'tis a venial slip.
But if I give my wife a handkerchief—

                                act 4, scene 1, lines 1–10

Lying naked in bed together is only a venial or pardonable slip, but then Iago brilliantly returns to the handkerchief. That trifle light as air becomes a scalpel carving Othello's soul.

Othello: What then?
Iago: Why then, 'tis hers, my lord, and being hers,
She may, I think, bestow't on any man.
Othello: She is protectress of her honor too.
May she give that?
Iago: Her honor is an essence that's not seen;
They have it very oft that have it not.
But, for the handkerchief—
Othello: By heaven, I would most gladly have forgot it.
Thou said'st—Oh, it comes o'er my memory
As doth the raven o'er the infectious house,

Boding to all—he had my handkerchief.

Iago: Ay, what of that?

Othello: That's not so good now.

act 4, scene 1, lines 11–23

Halting and sporadic, Othello's speech betrays a mental confusion so grave that he seems dehumanized. Iago surpasses himself in pressing home his poison:

Iago: What if I had said I had seen him do you wrong?

Or heard him say—as knaves be such abroad,

Who having, by their own importunate suit,

Or voluntary dotage of some mistress,

Convincèd or supplied them, cannot choose

But they must blab—

Othello: Hath he said anything?

Iago: He hath, my lord; but, be you well assured,

No more than he'll unswear.

Othello: What hath he said?

Iago: Faith, that he did—I know not what he did.

Othello: What? What?

Iago: Lie—

Othello: With her?

Iago: With her, on her; what you will.

Othello: Lie with her? Lie on her? We say "lie on her" when they belie her. Lie with her! Zounds, that's fulsome.—Handkerchief—confessions—handkerchief! To confess and be hanged for his labor—first to be hanged and

then to confess.—I tremble at it. Nature would not
invest herself in such shadowing passion without
some instruction. It is not words that shakes me thus.
Pish! Noses, ears, and lips.—Is't possible?—Confess—
handkerchief!—O devil!   *Falls in a trance.*

                    act 4, scene 1, lines 24–41

Iago's music of thought, discordant and merciless, annihilates the
Moor's remnant of composure. The refrain becomes "Lie," with the
double meaning of prevarication and intercourse. With brio, Iago
delivers his grand line: "With her, on her; what you will." Othello
five times repeats variations on "lie with her." "Fulsome!" is most foul.
"Handkerchief" is three times repeated by the Moor, as he threatens to hang Cassio before the lieutenant confesses. Othello's mind
is overcome as he loses control of fact. He insists that his fury means
Desdemona's guilt and that mere words could not shake him into
uncontrollable frenzy. As he faints into a trance, the images dance
in disorder: "Noses, ears, and lips," "handkerchief," and most sig-
nificantly "O devil!"—an unmeant yet accurate appellation for Iago.
Exuberant in aesthetic glee, Iago salutes his own elixir:

Work on,
My medicine, work! Thus credulous fools are caught,
And many worthy and chaste dames even thus,
All guiltless, meet reproach.—What, ho! My lord!
My lord, I say! Othello!

                        act 4, scene 1, lines 42–46

Shakespeare's singular power is to contaminate us with Iago's inventive joy. How many among us could withstand him? Frank Finlay so captivated me at this point that I was momentarily exuberant. Iago's manipulation of both Cassio and Othello is a work of genius:

> *Enter Cassio.*
> **Iago:** How now, Cassio?
> **Cassio:** What's the matter?
> **Iago:** My lord is fall'n into an epilepsy.
> This is his second fit. He had one yesterday.
> **Cassio:** Rub him about the temples.
> **Iago:** No, forbear.
> The lethargy must have his quiet course.
> If not, he foams at mouth, and by and by
> Breaks out to savage madness. Look, he stirs.
> Do you withdraw yourself a little while.
> He will recover straight. When he is gone,
> I would on great occasion speak with you.
> *Exit Cassio.*
>
> act 4, scene 1, lines 47–56

As an aesthetician of evil, Iago begins to run ahead of our apprehensions:

> **Iago:** How is it, General? Have you not hurt your head?
> **Othello:** Dost thou mock me?

Iago: I mock you not, by heaven.

Would you would bear your fortune like a man!

Othello: A hornèd man's a monster and a beast.

act 4, scene 1, lines 57–60

The Moor takes Iago's query as a reference to a cuckold's horns. The ancient seizes upon it to generalize with true gusto:

Iago: There's many a beast then in a populous city,

And many a civil monster.

Othello: Did he confess it?

Iago: Good sir, be a man.

Think every bearded fellow that's but yoked

May draw with you. There's millions now alive

That nightly lie in those unproper beds

Which they dare swear peculiar. Your case is better.

Oh, 'tis the spite of hell, the fiend's arch-mock,

To lip a wanton in a secure couch

And to suppose her chaste! No, let me know,

And knowing what I am, I know what she shall be.

Othello: O, thou art wise. 'Tis certain.

act 4, scene 1, lines 61–73

In this delightful vision, all married men are yoked to cuckoldry. They lie at night in beds not private to them, but at least Othello knows the facts. Iago is all for knowing. Emilia has cuckolded him, and she is a whore. Poor Othello whimpers in tribute to this wisdom.

Iago: Stand you a while apart;
Confine yourself but in a patient list.
Whilst you were here o'erwhelmed with your grief—
A passion most unsuiting such a man—
Cassio came hither. I shifted him away,
And laid good 'scuses upon your ecstasy,
Bade him anon return and here speak with me,
The which he promised. Do but encave yourself
And mark the fleers, the gibes, and notable scorns
That dwell in every region of his face;
For I will make him tell the tale anew,
Where, how, how oft, how long ago, and when
He hath and is again to cope your wife.
I say, but mark his gesture. Marry, patience!
Or I shall say you're all-in-all in spleen,
And nothing of a man.

Othello: Dost thou hear, Iago?
I will be found most cunning in my patience;
But—dost thou hear?—most bloody.

Iago: That's not amiss;
But yet keep time in all. Will you withdraw?
Othello stands apart.

act 4, scene 1, lines 74–92

Like a conductor, Iago commands Othello to maintain a steady beat. As a stage director, he urges the Moor to step aside. With the scene set, he teases Cassio about Bianca, so guiding his language that Othello will take the courtesan as being Desdemona:

Iago: Now will I question Cassio of Bianca,
A huswife that by selling her desires
Buys herself bread and clothes. It is a creature
That dotes on Cassio—as 'tis the strumpet's plague
To beguile many and be beguiled by one.
He, when he hears of her, cannot restrain
From the excess of laughter. Here he comes.

act 4, scene 1, lines 93–99

Iago's intimacy with us, the audience, transcends the easy villainy of Richard III. There is a spooky charm in his telling us "Now will I question Cassio of Bianca." The hussy Bianca has taken Cassio as her ponce, and the cheerful rapscallion responds with minimal affection and laughter.

Enter Cassio.
Iago: As he shall smile, Othello shall go mad;
And his unbookish jealousy must conster
Poor Cassio's smiles, gestures, and light behaviors
Quite in the wrong.—How do you now, Lieutenant?
Cassio: The worser that you give me the addition
Whose want even kills me.
Iago: Ply Desdemona well and you are sure on't.
[*Speaking lower*] Now, if this suit lay in Bianca's power,
How quickly should you speed!
Cassio: [*laughing*] Alas, poor caitiff!
Othello: [*aside*] Look how he laughs already!
Iago: I never knew woman love man so.

Cassio: Alas, poor rogue! I think, i'faith, she loves me.

Othello: [*aside*] Now he denies it faintly, and laughs it out.

Iago: Do you hear, Cassio?

Othello: [*aside*]   Now he importunes him
To tell it o'er. Go to! Well said, well said.

Iago: She gives it out that you shall marry her.
Do you intend it?

Cassio: Ha, ha, ha!

Othello: [*aside*] Do you triumph, Roman? Do you triumph?

Cassio: I marry her! What? A customer? Prithee, bear some charity
to my wit; do not think it so unwholesome. Ha, ha, ha!

Othello: [*aside*] So, so, so, so! They laugh that wins.

Iago: Faith, the cry goes that you marry her.

Cassio: Prithee say true.

Iago: I am a very villain else.

Othello: [*aside*] Have you scored me? Well.

Cassio: This is the monkey's own giving out. She is persuaded
I will marry her, out of her own love and flattery, not out
of my promise.

Othello: [*aside*] Iago beckons me. Now he begins the story.

Cassio: She was here even now; she haunts me in every place.
I was the other day talking on the seabank with certain
Venetians, and thither comes the bauble, and by this
hand, falls me thus about my neck— [*He embraces Iago.*]

Othello: [*aside*] Crying, "O dear Cassio!" as it were; his gesture
imports it.

Cassio: So hangs and lolls and weeps upon me, so shakes and
pulls me. Ha, ha, ha!

Othello: [*aside*] Now he tells how she plucked him to my
    chamber. Oh, I see that nose of yours, but not that dog I
    shall throw it to.
Cassio: Well, I must leave her company.

                      act 4, scene 1, lines 100–138

I cannot recall another effect like this in Shakespeare. It would be hilarious except that carnage beckons. The antiphonal to-and-fro of Cassio's lighthearted merriment with Othello's gathering fury produces an unsettling cacophony, rather as though Gilbert and Sullivan are being played against Boito and Verdi. Bianca's arrival with the inevitable handkerchief, though it could not have been overtly planned by Iago, sublimely fulfills his mission:

Iago: Before me, look where she comes.
Enter Bianca [*with Othello's handkerchief*].
Cassio: 'Tis such another fitchew! Marry, a perfumed one. —
    What do you mean by this haunting of me?

                      act 4, scene 1, lines 139–41

There is something deliciously self-gratulatory in Iago's "Before me, look where she comes." It is as though he calls out: "On my soul, here she is just when I need her." Ungallantly, Cassio terms poor Bianca a fitchew, or polecat—that is, a common whore.

Bianca: Let the devil and his dam haunt you! What did you
    mean by that same handkerchief you gave me even now?

I was a fine fool to take it. I must take out the work?
A likely piece of work, that you should find it in your
chamber and know not who left it there! This is some
minx's token, and I must take out the work? There; give
it your hobbyhorse. [*She gives him the handkerchief.*]
Wheresoever you had it, I'll take out no work on't.

Cassio: How now, my sweet Bianca? How now? How now?

Othello: [*aside*] By heaven, that should be my handkerchief!

act 4, scene 1, lines 142–50

Bianca plays on "a likely piece of work," at once a lying story,
a rival courtesan, and the fateful handkerchief. Othello descends
into rabidity, a mania for returning to chaos.

Bianca: If you'll come to supper tonight, you may; if you will
not, come when you are next prepared for.   *Exit.*

Iago: After her, after her.

Cassio: Faith, I must. She'll rail in the streets else.

Iago: Will you sup there?

Cassio: Faith, I intend so.

Iago: Well, I may chance to see you, for I would very fain
speak with you.

Cassio: Prithee come. Will you?

Iago: Go to. Say no more.

Exit Cassio.

act 4, scene 1, lines 151–59

With Cassio and Bianca removed, Iago turns to the kill:

Othello: [*advancing*]   How shall I murder him, Iago?

Iago: Did you perceive how he laughed at his vice?

Othello: Oh, Iago!

Iago: And did you see the handkerchief?

Othello: Was that mine?

Iago: Yours, by this hand. And to see how he prizes the foolish woman your wife! She gave it him, and he hath given it his whore.

Othello: I would have him nine years a-killing. A fine woman! A fair woman! A sweet woman!

Iago: Nay, you must forget that.

Othello: Ay, let her rot and perish, and be damned tonight, for she shall not live. No, my heart is turned to stone; I strike it, and it hurts my hand. Oh, the world hath not a sweeter creature! She might lie by an emperor's side and command him tasks.

Iago: Nay, that's not your way.

Othello: Hang her! I do but say what she is. So delicate with her needle! An admirable musician! Oh, she will sing the savageness out of a bear. Of so high and plenteous wit and invention!

Iago: She's the worse for all this.

Othello: Oh, a thousand, a thousand times! And then, of so gentle a condition!

Iago: Ay, too gentle.

Othello: Nay, that's certain. But yet the pity of it, Iago! Oh, Iago, the pity of it, Iago!

act 4, scene 1, lines 160–83

This heartbreaking crescendo scarcely can be borne. Even in his delirium, the Moor is overcome by appreciation for the wonder that is Desdemona. Iago—dramatist, director, and critic—instructs Othello that that is not the way to think about her. To Othello's plaintive exclamation that his wife is highborn and gentle, the critic Iago adds, "Ay, too gentle," that is, generously giving herself to other men.

Whenever I think about *Othello, the Moor of Venice*, I remember first that harrowing "But yet the pity of it, Iago! Oh, Iago, the pity of it, Iago!" And yet that pity shortly turns to monstrosity:

> Iago: If you are so fond over her iniquity, give her patent to
>   offend, for if it touch not you it comes near nobody.
> Othello: I will chop her into messes. Cuckold me!
>   act 4, scene 1, lines 184–86

It is a peculiar butchery for us to absorb; the pure warrior using his sword to chop his wife into so many portions of meat:

> Iago: Oh, 'tis foul in her.
> Othello: With mine officer?
> Iago: That's fouler.
> Othello: Get me some poison, Iago, this night. I'll not
>   expostulate with her, lest her body and beauty unprovide
>   my mind again. This night, Iago.
> Iago: Do it not with poison. Strangle her in her bed, even the
>   bed she hath contaminated.
> Othello: Good, good! The justice of it pleases. Very good.

Iago: And for Cassio, let me be his undertaker. You shall hear more by midnight.

Othello: Excellent good.

act 4, scene 1, lines 187–98

Writing with the lives of others, Iago usurps Shakespeare's function and chooses the manner of Desdemona's death. Cassio, he takes for himself. Shakespeare reassumes control with the call of a trumpet:

A trumpet within.

Othello: What trumpet is that same?

Iago: I warrant, something from Venice.

Enter Lodovico, Desdemona, and attendants.

'Tis Lodovico. This comes from the Duke.

See, your wife's with him.

Lodovico: God save you, worthy general!

Othello: With all my heart, sir.

Lodovico: [*giving him a letter*] The Duke and the Senators of Venice greet you.

Othello: I kiss the instrument of their pleasures.

[*He opens the letter and reads.*]

Desdemona: And what's the news, good cousin Lodovico?

Iago: I am very glad to see you, signor.

Welcome to Cyprus.

Lodovico: I thank you. How does Lieutenant Cassio?

Iago: Lives, sir.

Desdemona: Cousin, there's fall'n between him and my lord

An unkind breach; but you shall make all well.

Othello: Are you sure of that?

Desdemona: My lord?

Othello: [*reads*] "This fail you not to do, as you will—"

Lodovico: He did not call; he's busy in the paper.

Is there division 'twixt my lord and Cassio?

Desdemona: A most unhappy one. I would do much

T'atone them, for the love I bear to Cassio.

Othello: Fire and brimstone!

Desdemona: My lord?

Othello: Are you wise?

Desdemona: What, is he angry?

Lodovico: May be the letter moved him;

For, as I think, they do command him home,

Deputing Cassio in his government.

Desdemona: By my troth, I am glad on't.

Othello: Indeed?

Desdemona: My lord?

Othello: I am glad to see you mad.

act 4, scene 1, lines 198–229

That monosyllabic line, with its interior rhyme, is a death knell. Desdemona's innocent joy is answered by Othello's "how happy I am that you are insane enough to rejoice in your lover's promotion."

Desdemona: Why, sweet Othello—

Othello: [*striking her*] Devil!

Desdemona: I have not deserved this.

Lodovico: My lord, this would not be believed in Venice,

Though I should swear I saw't. 'Tis very much.

Make her amends, she weeps.

Othello: O devil, devil!

If that the earth could teem with woman's tears,

Each drop she falls would prove a crocodile.

Out of my sight!

Desdemona: I will not stay to offend you.   [*Going.*]

Lodovico: Truly, an obedient lady.

I do beseech Your Lordship call her back.

Othello: [*calling*] Mistress!

Desdemona: [*returning*] My lord?

Othello: What would you with her, sir?

Lodovico: Who, I, my lord?

Othello: Ay, you did wish that I would make her turn.

Sir, she can turn, and turn, and yet go on

And turn again; and she can weep, sir, weep;

And she's obedient, as you say, obedient,

Very obedient.—Proceed you in your tears.—

Concerning this, sir—Oh, well-painted passion!—

I am commanded home.—Get you away;

I'll send for you anon.—Sir, I obey the mandate,

And will return to Venice.—Hence, avaunt!   [*Exit*

        Desdemona.]

Cassio shall have my place. And, sir, tonight

I do entreat that we may sup together.

You are welcome, sir, to Cyprus.—Goats and monkeys!

                        act 4, scene 1, lines 230–56

90

The three "turns" are sexual innuendos, as are the three "obe-dients." The cry of "Goats and monkeys!" echoes Iago. Lodovico's rhetorical questions mark the end of Othello:

Lodovico: Is this the noble Moor whom our full Senate

Call all in all sufficient? Is this the nature

Whom passion could not shake? Whose solid virtue

The shot of accident nor dart of chance

Could neither graze nor pierce?

Iago: He is much changed.

Lodovico: Are his wits safe? Is he not light of brain?

Iago: He's that he is. I may not breathe my censure

What he might be. If what he might he is not,

I would to heaven he were!

Lodovico: What! Strike his wife!

Iago: Faith, that was not so well; yet would I knew

That stroke would prove the worst!

Lodovico: Is it his use?

Or did the letters work upon his blood

And new-create this fault?

Iago: Alas, alas!

It is not honesty in me to speak

What I have seen and known. You shall observe him,

And his own courses will denote him so

That I may save my speech. Do but go after

And mark how he continues.

Lodovico: I am sorry that I am deceived in him.

act 4, scene 1, lines 257–75

Iago's dry "He is much changed" leads to Lodovico's wonder as to the Moor's sanity. Iago, citing his own honesty, implies that it would indeed be better if Othello were mad, since only that could condone his outrageousness. With Lodovico, all of us are sorry that we were deceived by the Moor's former greatness.

CHAPTER 7

I Understand a Fury
in Your Words, /
But Not the Words

We go from the space before the citadel to its interior, where Othello confronts Emilia:

> **Othello:** You have seen nothing, then?
> **Emilia:** Nor ever heard, nor ever did suspect.
> **Othello:** Yes, you have seen Cassio and her together.
> **Emilia:** But then I saw no harm, and then I heard
> Each syllable that breath made up between them.
> **Othello:** What? Did they never whisper?
> **Emilia:** Never, my lord.
> **Othello:** Nor send you out o'th'way?
> **Emilia:** Never.
> **Othello:** To fetch her fan, her gloves, her mask, nor nothing?
> **Emilia:** Never, my lord.
> **Othello:** That's strange.
>
> act 4, scene 2, lines 1–12

At the edge of again going berserk, Othello cannot accept the truth. Emilia, who is true gold, does her best but nothing avails:

Emilia: I durst, my lord, to wager she is honest,
Lay down my soul at stake. If you think other,
Remove your thought; it doth abuse your bosom.
If any wretch have put this in your head,
Let heaven requite it with the serpent's curse!
For if she be not honest, chaste, and true,
There's no man happy; the purest of their wives
Is foul as slander.
Othello: Bid her come hither. Go.   *Exit Emilia.*
She says enough; yet she's a simple bawd
That cannot say as much. This is a subtle whore,
A closet lock and key of villainous secrets.
And yet she'll kneel and pray; I have seen her do't.

                                        act 4, scene 2, lines 13–24

The Moor is beyond accurate hearing. Viciously he tells himself that any procuress could say the same. Desdemona is merely a subtle whore, hiding her erotic secrets and given to kneeling and praying:

Enter Desdemona and Emilia.
Desdemona: My lord, what is your will?
Othello: Pray you, chuck, come hither.
Desdemona: What is your pleasure?
Othello: Let me see your eyes;

Look in my face.

Desdemona: What horrible fancy's this?

Othello: [*to Emilia*] Some of your function, mistress.

Leave procreants alone and shut the door;

Cough, or cry "hem," if anybody come.

Your mystery, your mystery! Nay, dispatch.   *Exit Emilia.*

Desdemona: [*kneeling*]

Upon my knees, what doth your speech import?

I understand a fury in your words,

But not the words.

act 4, scene 2, lines 25–35

Emilia is dismissed to practice her mystery or trade of watching the door like a bawd. Desdemona, abjectly kneeling, precisely comprehends her husband's rage but not its cause. What follows is both incredibly painful and yet eloquent, in the wake of Iago's instruction:

Othello: Why, what art thou?

Desdemona: Your wife, my lord, your true

And loyal wife.

Othello: Come swear it, damn thyself,

Lest, being like one of heaven, the devils themselves

Should fear to seize thee. Therefore be double damned:

Swear thou art honest.

Desdemona: Heaven doth truly know it.

Othello: Heaven truly knows that thou art false as hell.

Desdemona: To whom, my lord? With whom? How am I false?

Othello: [*weeping*] Ah! Desdemon! Away, away, away!
Desdemona: Alas the heavy day! Why do you weep?
Am I the motive of these tears, my lord?
If haply you my father do suspect
An instrument of this your calling back,
Lay not your blame on me. If you have lost him,
Why, I have lost him too.

act 4, scene 2, lines 36–49

The Moor grants that she looks like an angel but is hellish. When he breaks into tears, it is unbearable to the audience that Desdemona seeks to comfort him. And then he continues to break apart:

Othello: Had it pleased heaven
To try me with affliction, had they rained
All kind of sores and shames on my bare head,
Steeped me in poverty to the very lips,
Given to captivity me and my utmost hopes,
I should have found in some place of my soul
A drop of patience. But, alas, to make me
The fixèd figure for the time of scorn
To point his slow unmoving finger at!
Yet could I bear that too, well, very well.
But there where I have garnered up my heart,
Where either I must live or bear no life,
The fountain from the which my current runs
Or else dries up—to be discarded thence!

Or keep it as a cistern for foul toads
To knot and gender in! Turn thy complexion there,
Patience, thou young and rose-lipped cherubin—
Ay, there look grim as hell!
Desdemona: I hope my noble lord esteems me honest.
Othello: O ay; as summer flies are in the shambles,
That quicken even with blowing. O thou weed,
Who art so lovely fair and smell'st so sweet
That the sense aches at thee, would thou hadst ne'er been born!
                                          act 4, scene 2, lines 49–71

The moral ugliness of the Moor makes us wonder whether his wounded dignity outweighs his love. Invective pours from him as though he has become a cesspool, despite his imagery of fountain or fresh spring. The disproportion between his uncontrollable rhetoric and the blameless Desdemona surpasses all measure:

Desdemona: Alas, what ignorant sin have I committed?
Othello: Was this fair paper, this most goodly book,
Made to write "whore" upon? What committed?
Committed? O thou public commoner!
I should make very forges of my cheeks,
That would to cinders burn up modesty,
Did I but speak thy deeds. What committed?
Heaven stops the nose at it and the moon winks;
The bawdy wind, that kisses all it meets
Is hushed within the hollow mine of earth,
And will not hear't. What committed?

Impudent strumpet!

Desdemona: By heaven, you do me wrong.

act 4, scene 2, lines 72–83

Heroically braving this barrage, Desdemona invokes heaven against the Moor's slanders.

Othello: Are not you a strumpet?

Desdemona: No, as I am a Christian.
If to preserve this vessel for my lord
From any other foul unlawful touch
Be not to be a strumpet, I am none.

Othello: What, not a whore?

Desdemona: No, as I shall be saved.

Othello: Is't possible?

Desdemona: O, heaven forgive us!

Othello: I cry you mercy, then.
I took you for that cunning whore of Venice
That married with Othello. [*Calling out*] You, mistress,
That have the office opposite to Saint Peter
And keeps the gate of hell!
Enter Emilia.

                    You, you, ay, you!
We have done our course. There's money for your pains.
I pray you, turn the key and keep our counsel.   *Exit.*

act 4, scene 2, lines 84–98

"We have done our course" obscenely implies that Othello's rant is an erotic escapade. Yet there are darker overtones, preluding murder. The decline and fall of the Moor possesses a violence from within that assaults the audience beyond the limit of endurance. Not only is Othello's catastrophe incredibly painful, Shakespeare draws it out at excruciating length. Iago gets inside us. We can fight against him, but his sadism becomes ours:

Emilia: Alas, what does this gentleman conceive?
How do you, madam? How do you, my good lady?
Desdemona: Faith, half asleep.
Emilia: Good madam, what's the matter with my lord?
Desdemona: With who?
Emilia: Why, with my lord, madam.
Desdemona: Who is thy lord?
Emilia: He that is yours, sweet lady.
Desdemona: I have none. Do not talk to me, Emilia.
I cannot weep, nor answers have I none,
But what should go by water. Prithee, tonight
Lay on my bed my wedding sheets—remember;
And call thy husband hither.
Emilia: Here's a change indeed!   *Exit.*
Desdemona: 'Tis meet I should be used so, very meet.
How have I been behaved, that he might stick
The small'st opinion on my least misuse?

                    act 4, scene 2, lines 99–114

Dazed, Desdemona holds back her tears and tries to believe that somehow she has deserved this anguish. The wedding sheets will remain virginal and presage her terrible end. Iago prolongs his triumph:

Enter Iago and Emilia.
Iago: What is your pleasure, madam? How is't with you?
Desdemona: I cannot tell. Those that do teach young babes
Do it with gentle means and easy tasks.
He might have chid me so, for, in good faith,
I am a child to chiding.

act 4, scene 2, lines 115–19

The intricate music of "chid," "child," "chiding" begins her requiem.

Iago: What is the matter, lady?
Emilia: Alas, Iago, my lord hath so bewhored her,
Thrown such despite and heavy terms upon her,
That true hearts cannot bear it.
Desdemona: Am I that name, Iago?
Iago: What name, fair lady?
Desdemona: Such as she said my lord did say I was.
Emilia: He called her whore. A beggar in his drink
Could not have laid such terms upon his callet.

act 4, scene 2, lines 120–28

A "callet" is a low-class whore. Emilia's outrage is cleansing yet dangerous to her life.

Iago: Why did he so?

Desdemona: [*weeping*] I do not know. I am sure I am none
  such.

Iago: Do not weep, do not weep. Alas the day!

Emilia: Hath she forsook so many noble matches,

Her father and her country and her friends,

To be called whore? Would it not make one weep?

Desdemona: It is my wretched fortune.

Iago: Beshrew him for't!

How comes this trick upon him?

Desdemona: Nay, heaven doth know.

Emilia: I will be hanged if some eternal villain,

Some busy and insinuating rogue,

Some cogging, cozening slave, to get some office,

Have not devised this slander. I'll be hanged else.

act 4, scene 2, lines 129–40

Emilia's awakening is something radically new. Shakespeare
revises so as to enhance her role.

Iago: Fie, there is no such man. It is impossible.

Desdemona: If any such there be, heaven pardon him!

Emilia: A halter pardon him! And hell gnaw his bones!

Why should he call her whore? Who keeps her company?

What place? What time? What form? What likelihood?

The Moor's abused by some most villainous knave,

Some base notorious knave, some scurvy fellow.

Oh, heavens, that such companions thou'dst unfold,

And put in every honest hand a whip
To lash the rascals naked through the world
Even from the east to th'west!
Iago: Speak within door.

act 4, scene 2, lines 141–51

Iago hushes her but senses she is beyond his control.

Emilia: O fie upon them! Some such squire he was
That turned your wit the seamy side without
And made you to suspect me with the Moor.
Iago: You are a fool. Go to.
Desdemona: O God, Iago,
What shall I do to win my lord again?
Good friend, go to him; for, by this light of heaven,
I know not how I lost him. Here I kneel.
If e'er my will did trespass 'gainst his love,
Either in discourse of thought or actual deed,
Or that mine eyes, mine ears, or any sense
Delighted them in any other form;
Or that I do not yet, and ever did,
And ever will—though he do shake me off
To beggarly divorcement—love him dearly,
Comfort forswear me! Unkindness may do much,
And his unkindness may defeat my life,
But never taint my love. I cannot say "whore."
It does abhor me now I speak the word;

To do the act that might the addition earn
Not the world's mass of vanity could make me.

act 4, scene 2, lines 152–71

Shakespeare's uncanny ear gives us the sequence: "whore,"
"abhor," "word."

Iago: I pray you be content. 'Tis but his humor.
The business of the state does him offense,
And he does chide with you.
Desdemona: If 'twere no other—
Iago: It is but so, I warrant.   [*Trumpets within.*]
Hark how these instruments summon to supper!
The messengers of Venice stays the meat.
Go in, and weep not. All things shall be well.
Exeunt Desdemona and Emilia.

act 4, scene 2, lines 172–79

"All things shall be well" signifies nothing but Iago's triumphalism. He proceeds to the further gulling of Roderigo:

Iago: But, Roderigo, if thou hast that in thee indeed which I
have greater reason to believe now than ever—I mean
purpose, courage, and valor—this night show it. If thou
the next night following enjoy not Desdemona, take me
from this world with treachery and devise engines for
my life.

103

Roderigo: Well, what is it? Is it within reason and compass?

Iago: Sir, there is especial commission come from Venice to depute Cassio in Othello's place.

Roderigo: Is that true? Why then Othello and Desdemona return again to Venice.

Iago: Oh, no; he goes into Mauritania and takes away with him the fair Desdemona, unless his abode be lingered here by some accident; wherein none can be so determinate as the removing of Cassio.

Roderigo: How do you mean, removing him?

Iago: Why, by making him uncapable of Othello's place— knocking out his brains.

Roderigo: And that you would have me to do?

Iago: Ay, if you dare do yourself a profit and a right. He sups tonight with a harlotry, and thither will I go to him— he knows not yet of his honorable fortune. If you will watch his going thence, which I will fashion to fall out between twelve and one, you may take him at your pleasure. I will be near to second your attempt, and he shall fall between us. Come, stand not amazed at it, but go along with me. I will show you such a necessity in his death that you shall think yourself bound to put it on him. It is now high suppertime, and the night grows to waste. About it.

Roderigo: I will hear further reason for this.

Iago: And you shall be satisfied.

Exeunt.

act 4, scene 2, lines 214–40

William Hazlitt, the great English Romantic literary critic, in his *Characters of Shakespeare's Plays* (1817), best characterizes Iago:

"Our ancient" is a philosopher, who fancies that a lie that kills has more point in it than an alliteration or an antithesis; who thinks a fatal experiment on the peace of a family a better thing than watching the palpitations in the heart of a flea in a microscope; who plots the ruin of his friends as an exercise for his ingenuity, and stabs men in the dark to prevent *ennui*.

That will be the fate of Roderigo and very nearly of Cassio. But first we return to the citadel and to Othello, Desdemona, Emilia, and Lodovico:

Lodovico: I do beseech you, sir, trouble yourself no further.
Othello: Oh, pardon me; 'twill do me good to walk.
Lodovico: Madam, good night; I humbly thank Your
     Ladyship.
Desdemona: Your Honor is most welcome.
Othello: Will you walk, sir?
Oh, Desdemona!
Desdemona: My lord?
Othello: Get you to bed on th'instant; I will be returned
     forthwith. Dismiss your attendant there. Look't be done.
Desdemona: I will, my lord.
Exit Othello, with Lodovico and attendants.

                        act 4, scene 3, lines 1–9

The agonizing death march of Desdemona proceeds. Once again I wonder at Shakespeare's protracted harrowing of the audience. There is a lyrical splendor in the farewell ceremony of Emilia's preparing of Desdemona for bed that jars our nerves as the slaughter impends:

Emilia: How goes it now? He looks gentler than he did.

Desdemona: He says he will return incontinent,

And hath commanded me to go to bed,

And bid me to dismiss you.

Emilia: Dismiss me?

Desdemona: It was his bidding. Therefore, good Emilia,

Give me my nightly wearing, and adieu.

We must not now displease him.

Emilia: I would you had never seen him!

Desdemona: So would not I. My love doth so approve him

That even his stubbornness, his checks, his frowns—

Prithee, unpin me—have grace and favor in them.

[*Emilia prepares Desdemona for bed.*]

Emilia: I have laid those sheets you bade me on the bed.

Desdemona: All's one. Good faith, how foolish are our minds!

If I do die before thee, prithee, shroud me

In one of those same sheets.

Emilia: Come, come, you talk.

act 4, scene 3, lines 10–25

"Incontinent" means immediately. Desdemona, sublime in her love for the Moor, values even his roughness and insults. The wedding sheets are on the bed, and Desdemona wonders if it really matters. Precariously she requests burial in one of the sheets, and Emilia tries to dismiss this foreboding. Shakespeare's subtle cunning gives us the contention between Desdemona's song of sorrowful love and a momentary impulse pondering her own unlived life:

> Desdemona: My mother had a maid called Barbary.
> She was in love, and he she loved proved mad
> And did forsake her. She had a song of "Willow."
> An old thing 'twas, but it expressed her fortune,
> And she died singing it. That song tonight
> Will not go from my mind; I have much to do
> But to go hang my head all at one side
> And sing it like poor Barbary. Prithee, dispatch.
>
> act 4, scene 3, lines 26–33

The faithless lover was a wild man, and Barbary dies singing the willow song, traditional for thwarted love. Musing on the handsome Lodovico, who would have been the proper bridegroom for her, Desdemona implicitly realizes she will share Barbary's fate:

> Emilia: Shall I go fetch your nightgown?
> Desdemona: No, unpin me here.
> This Lodovico is a proper man.
> Emilia: A very handsome man.
> Desdemona: He speaks well.
> Emilia: I know a lady in Venice would have walked barefoot to
>   Palestine for a touch of his nether lip.
> Desdemona: [*singing*]

"The poor soul sat sighing by a sycamore tree,
Sing all a green willow;
Her hand on her bosom, her head on her knee,
Sing willow, willow, willow.
The fresh streams ran by her and murmured her moans;
Sing willow, willow, willow;
Her salt tears fell from her, and softened the stones—"

Lay by these.
[*singing*] "Sing willow, willow, willow—"
Prithee hie thee. He'll come anon.

[*singing*] "Sing all a green willow must be my garland.
Let nobody blame him, his scorn I approve—"

Nay, that's not next.—Hark! who is't that knocks?
Emilia: It's the wind.
Desdemona: [*singing*]

"I called my love false love; but what said he then?
Sing willow, willow, willow;
If I court more women, you'll couch with more men."

So get thee gone; good night. Mine eyes do itch;
Doth that bode weeping?
Emilia: 'Tis neither here nor there.
Desdemona: I have heard it said so. Oh, these men, these men!
Dost thou in conscience think—tell me—Emilia,

That there be women do abuse their husbands
In such gross kind?
Emilia: There be some such, no question.
Desdemona: Wouldst thou do such a deed for all the world?
Emilia: Why, would not you?
Desdemona: No, by this heavenly light!
Emilia: Nor I neither by this heavenly light;
I might do't as well i'th'dark.

act 4, scene 3, lines 34–67

A free spirit, Emilia is a truth-teller.

Desdemona: Wouldst thou do such a deed for all the world?
Emilia: The world's a huge thing. 'Tis is a great price
For a small vice.
Desdemona: Good troth, I think thou wouldst not.
Emilia: By my troth, I think I should, and undo't when I had
    done. Marry, I would not do such a thing for a joint
    ring, nor for measures of lawn, nor for gowns, petticoats,
    nor caps, nor any petty exhibition. But, for all the whole
    world! Uds pity, who would not make her husband
    a cuckold to make him a monarch? I should venture
    purgatory for't.
Desdemona: Beshrew me if I would do such a wrong
For the whole world.
Emilia: Why, the wrong is but a wrong i'th'world, and having
    the world for your labor, 'tis a wrong in your own world,
    and you might quickly make it right.

Desdemona: I do not think there is any such woman.

Emilia: Yes, a dozen, and as many
To th'vantage as would store the world they played for.
But I do think it is their husbands' faults
If wives do fall. Say that they slack their duties,
And pour our treasures into foreign laps,
Or else break out in peevish jealousies,
Throwing restraint upon us? Or say they strike us,
Or scant our former having in despite?
Why, we have galls, and though we have some grace,
Yet have we some revenge. Let husbands know
Their wives have sense like them. They see, and smell,
And have their palates both for sweet and sour,
As husbands have. What is it that they do
When they change us for others? Is it sport?
I think it is. And doth affection breed it?
I think it doth. Is't frailty that thus errs?
It is so, too. And have not we affections,
Desires for sport, and frailty, as men have?
Then let them use us well; else let them know,
The ills we do, their ills instruct us so.

Desdemona: Good night, good night. God me such uses send
Not to pick bad from bad, but by bad mend!   *Exeunt.*

act 4, scene 3, lines 68–104

Iago, both jealous and impotent, has aroused Emilia to a strong defense of maltreated wives, one that at last must undo him. Desdemona declines the lesson and is too good to live.

On a Cyprus street, Iago stage-manages what he hopes will be the double immolation of Roderigo and Cassio:

> **Iago:** I have rubbed this young quat almost to the sense,
> And he grows angry. Now, whether he kill Cassio
> Or Cassio him, or each do kill the other,
> Every way makes my gain. Live Roderigo,
> He calls me to a restitution large
> Of gold and jewels that I bobbed from him
> As gifts to Desdemona.
> It must not be. If Cassio do remain,
> He hath a daily beauty in his life
> That makes me ugly; and besides, the Moor
> May unfold me to him; there stand I in much peril.
> No, he must die. Be't so. I hear him coming.
>
> act 5, scene 1, lines 9–20

A quat is a pimple, an apt description for Roderigo, rubbed to bursting. Iago's inward motion reveals more than a sense of injured merit. Instead it manifests a Satanic resentment of Cassio's daily beauty or fundamental goodness that contrasts to the ancient's ugliness. More crucial is the risk that Othello, should he learn the truth, will kill Iago.

Enter Cassio.

Roderigo: [*coming forth*] I know his gait, 'tis he.—Villain, thou
      diest!   [*He attacks Cassio.*]
Cassio: That thrust had been mine enemy indeed,

But that my coat is better than thou know'st;

I will make proof of thine.   [*He draws, and*

    wounds Roderigo.]

Roderigo: O, I am slain!

[*He falls. Iago, from behind, wounds Cassio in the leg, and exits.*]

Cassio: I am maimed forever. Help, ho! Murder! Murder!

                act 5, scene 1, lines 23–27

Stabbing from behind, Iago's mode, will be repeated shortly.

Enter Othello.

Othello: The voice of Cassio! Iago keeps his word.

Roderigo: Oh, villain that I am!

Othello: It is even so.

Cassio: O, help, ho! Light! A surgeon!

Othello: 'Tis he: O brave Iago, honest and just,

That hast such noble sense of thy friend's wrong!

Thou teachest me.—Minion, your dear lies dead,

And your unblest fate hies. Strumpet, I come!

Forth of my heart those charms, thine eyes, are blotted;

Thy bed, lust-stained, shall with lust's blood be spotted.

                Exit Othello.

                act 5, scene 1, lines 28–37

It seems scarcely conceivable that the Moor could ever rise from this nadir. He might as well be Aaron the Moor in *Titus Andronicus*, Shakespeare's early send-up of the tragedies of blood. Perhaps only Shakespeare could find a way, at the close, to make Othello even a touch sympathetic.

Enter Lodovico and Gratiano.

Cassio: What, ho! No watch? No passage? Murder! Murder!

Gratiano: 'Tis some mischance. The voice is very direful.

Cassio: Oh, help!

Lodovico: Hark!

Roderigo: Oh wretched villain!

Lodovico: Two or three groan. 'Tis heavy night;

These may be counterfeits. Let's think't unsafe

To come in to the cry without more help.

[*They remain near the entrance.*]

Roderigo: Nobody come? Then shall I bleed to death.

Enter Iago [in his shirtsleeves, with a light].

Lodovico: Hark!

Gratiano: Here's one comes in his shirt, with light and
weapons.

Iago: Who's there? Whose noise is this that cries on murder?

Lodovico: We do not know.

Iago: Did not you hear a cry?

Cassio: Here, here! For heaven's sake, help me!

Iago: What's the matter?

[*He moves toward Cassio.*]

Gratiano: [*to Lodovico*] This is Othello's ancient, as I take it.

Lodovico: [*to Gratiano*] The same indeed, a very valiant fellow.

Iago: [*to Cassio*] What are you here that cry so grievously?

Cassio: Iago? Oh, I am spoiled, undone by villains!

Give me some help.

Iago: Oh, me, Lieutenant! What villains have done this?

Cassio: I think that one of them is hereabout,

And cannot make away.

Iago: Oh, treacherous villains! [*To Lodovico and Gratiano*]

    What are you there? Come in, and give some help.

Roderigo: Oh, help me there!

Cassio: That's one of them.

Iago: Oh, murderous slave! Oh, villain!

                        [*He stabs Roderigo.*]

Roderigo: Oh, damned Iago! Oh, inhuman dog!

Iago: Kill men i'th'dark?—Where be these bloody thieves?—

How silent is this town!—Ho! Murder, murder!—

[*To Lodovico and Gratiano*] What may you be? Are you of

    good or evil?

                        act 5, scene 1, lines 38–66

This is William Hazlitt's ancient, stabbing in the dark and thoroughly enjoying his own zestful release from boredom.

Lodovico: As you shall prove us, praise us.

Iago: Signor Lodovico?

Lodovico: He, sir.

Iago: I cry you mercy. Here's Cassio hurt by villains.

Gratiano: Cassio?

Iago: How is't, brother?

Cassio: My leg is cut in two.

Iago: Marry, heaven forbid!
Light, gentlemen! I'll bind it with my shirt.
[*He hands them the light, and tends to Cassio's wound.*]

act 5, scene 1, lines 67–76

Nothing if not critical, Iago continues to elaborate his night-piece. He gratuitously implicates Bianca and utters a grand aside: "This is the night / That either makes me or fordoes me quite." It accomplishes both.

CHAPTER 8

From This Time Forth
I Never Will Speak Word

Enter Othello [with a light], and Desdemona in her bed.
Othello: It is the cause, it is the cause, my soul.
Let me not name it to you, you chaste stars!
It is the cause. Yet I'll not shed her blood,
Nor scar that whiter skin of hers than snow,
And smooth as monumental alabaster.

act 5, scene 2, lines 1–5

Frenzied and bewildered, the Moor repeats "the cause" three times. He does not know what it means, nor do we. Is it the reason for impending slaughter? Or is it a barbaric principle? Either way, Othello is made more dreadful by his vow to keep his wife's beauty unblemished by strangling her.

Yet she must die, else she'll betray more men.
Put out the light, and then put out the light.
If I quench thee, thou flaming minister,

I can again thy former light restore,

Should I repent me; but once put out thy light,

Thou cunning'st pattern of excelling nature,

I know not where is that Promethean heat

That can thy light relume. When I have plucked thy rose,

I cannot give it vital growth again;

It needs must wither. I'll smell thee on the tree.   [*He kisses her*]

O balmy breath, that dost almost persuade

Justice to break her sword! One more, one more.

Be thus when thou art dead, and I will kill thee

And love thee after. One more, and this the last. [*He kisses her*]

So sweet was ne'er so fatal. I must weep,

But they are cruel tears. This sorrow's heavenly;

It strikes where it doth love. She wakes.

act 5, scene 2, lines 6–22

The peculiar monstrosity of this eros is that the Moor, once the master of separating the camp of war from that of peace, is lost in a whirligig of violence and affection.

Desdemona: Who's there? Othello?

Othello: Ay, Desdemona.

Desdemona: Will you come to bed, my lord?

Othello: Have you prayed tonight, Desdemon?

Desdemona: Ay, my lord.

Othello: If you bethink yourself of any crime

Unreconciled as yet to heaven and grace,

Solicit for it straight.

Desdemona: Alack, my lord, what may you mean by that?

Othello: Well, do it, and be brief. I will walk by.

I would not kill thy unpreparèd spirit.

No, heaven forfend! I would not kill thy soul.

Desdemona: Talk you of killing?

Othello: Ay, I do.

Desdemona: Then heaven

Have mercy on me!

Othello: Amen, with all my heart!

Desdemona: If you say so, I hope you will not kill me.

Othello: Humh!

Desdemona: And yet I fear you; for you're fatal then

When your eyes roll so. Why I should fear I know not,

Since guiltiness I know not; but yet I feel I fear.

Othello: Think on thy sins.

Desdemona: They are loves I bear to you.

                              act 5, scene 2, lines 23–42

The appalling pathos is in her accuracy. Her only sins were her mistaken passion for the Moor and her loyalty to him.

Othello: Ay, and for that thou diest.

Desdemona: That death's unnatural that kills for loving.

Alas, why gnaw you so your nether lip?

Some bloody passion shakes your very frame.

These are portents; but yet, I hope, I hope,

119

They do not point on me.
Othello: Peace, and be still!
Desdemona: I will so. What's the matter?

act 5, scene 2, lines 43–50

When I stand back from *Othello, the Moor of Venice*, what I remember best is the projected torment that Shakespeare inflicts upon us. Only the tragedy of *King Lear* rivals our suffering. And yet with *King Lear* a world shatters. In *Othello*, a marvelous woman, blameless and exquisite, is destroyed. It may be that the end of a nation ought to outweigh an individual martyrdom, yet the sublimity of Lear's tragedy is beyond us. Desdemona is within our capacity to feel and grieve.

Othello: That handkerchief which I so loved, and gave thee
Thou gav'st to Cassio.
Desdemona: No, by my life and soul!
Send for the man and ask him.
Othello: Sweet soul, take heed, take heed of perjury.
Thou art on thy deathbed.
Desdemona: Ay, but not yet to die.
Othello: Yes, presently.
Therefore confess thee freely of thy sin;
For to deny each article with oath
Cannot remove nor choke the strong conception
That I do groan withal. Thou art to die.

act 5, scene 2, lines 51–60

Shakespeare does not spare us the irony of "choke." "Conception" is both the Moor's purposed butchery and the bringing to birth, with appropriate groans, of his mania.

Desdemona: Then Lord have mercy on me!

Othello: I say, amen.

Desdemona: And have you mercy too! I never did

Offend you in my life; never loved Cassio

But with such general warranty of heaven

As I might love. I never gave him token.

Othello: By heaven, I saw my handkerchief in 's hand.

O perjured woman! Thou dost stone my heart,

And makes me call what I intend to do

A murder, which I thought a sacrifice.

I saw the handkerchief.

Desdemona: He found it, then.

I never gave it him. Send for him hither;

Let him confess a truth.

Othello: He had confessed.

Desdemona: What, my lord?

Othello: That he hath used thee.

Desdemona: How? Unlawfully?

Othello: Ay.

Desdemona: He will not say so.

Othello: No, his mouth is stopped;

Honest Iago hath ta'en order for't.

Desdemona: Oh, my fear interprets. What, is he dead?

Othello: Had all his hairs been lives, my great revenge
Had stomach for them all.
Desdemona: Alas, he is betrayed and I undone!   [*She weeps.*]

act 5, scene 2, lines 61–80

The rhythm of this is inexorable. Relentlessly, Shakespeare presses on:

Othello: Out, strumpet! Weep'st thou for him to my face?
Desdemona: Oh, banish me, my lord, but kill me not!
Othello: Down, strumpet!
Desdemona: Kill me tomorrow; let me live tonight!
Othello: Nay, if you strive—
Desdemona: But half an hour!
Othello: Being done, there is no pause.
Desdemona: But while I say one prayer!
Othello: It is too late.   *Smothers her.*
Emilia: [*at the door*] My lord, my lord! What, ho! My lord, my
      lord!
Othello: What noise is this? Not dead? Not yet quite dead?
I that am cruel am yet merciful;
I would not have thee linger in thy pain.   [*He dispatches her.*]
So, so.

act 5, scene 2, lines 81–92

Nothing mitigates Othello's crime. Pathologically, he is lost in the abyss of self to which Iago reduced him. Shakespeare frightens us with imagery of earthquake and eclipses:

Emilia: [*within*] What, ho! My lord, my lord!

Othello: Who's there?

Emilia: [*within*] O, good my lord, I would speak a word with
    you!

Othello: Yes, 'tis Emilia.—By and by.—She's dead.

'Tis like she comes to speak of Cassio's death.—

The noise was high. Ha! No more moving?

                                        act 5, scene 2, lines 93–96

The Folio reads "high" but many editors prefer the Quarto "here."

Othello: Still as the grave. Shall she come in? Were't good?—

I think she stirs again. No. What's best to do?

If she come in, she'll sure speak to my wife.

My wife! My wife! What wife? I have no wife.

Oh, insupportable! Oh, heavy hour!

Methinks it should be now a huge eclipse

Of sun and moon, and that th'affrighted globe

Did yawn at alteration.

The horrified globe opens wide, as in an earthquake, confronting simultaneous lunar and solar eclipses.

Emilia: [*within*]   I do beseech you

That I may speak with you, oh, good my lord!

Othello: I had forgot thee. Oh, come in, Emilia.—

Soft, by and by. Let me the curtains draw.—

[*He closes the bedcurtains and opens the door.*]

Where art thou?

Enter Emilia.

What's the matter with thee now?

Emilia: O, my good lord, yonder's foul murders done!

Othello: What, now?

Emilia: But now, my lord.

Othello: It is the very error of the moon;

She comes more nearer earth than she was wont,

And makes men mad.

Emilia: Cassio, my lord, hath killed a young Venetian

Called Roderigo.

Othello: Roderigo killed?

And Cassio killed?

Emilia: No, Cassio is not killed.

Othello: Not Cassio killed? Then murder's out of tune,

And sweet revenge grows harsh.

Desdemona: O, falsely, falsely murdered!

Emilia: O Lord, what cry is that?

Othello: That? What?

Emilia: Out, and alas, that was my lady's voice.

[She opens the bedcurtains.]

Help, help, ho, help! O lady, speak again!

Sweet Desdemona! O sweet mistress, speak!

Desdemona: A guiltless death I die.

Emilia: Oh, who hath done this deed?

Desdemona: Nobody; I myself. Farewell.

Commend me to my kind lord. Oh, farewell!   *[She dies.]*

act 5, scene 2, lines 97–129

In our shock, we scarcely can wonder how someone smothered to death revives sufficiently to make three more statements. We are swept on to Othello's confused agony:

Othello: Why, how should she be murdered?
Emilia: Alas, who knows?
Othello: You heard her say herself it was not I.
Emilia: She said so. I must needs report the truth.
Othello: She's like a liar gone to burning hell!
'Twas I that killed her.
Emilia: Oh, the more angel she,
And you the blacker devil!
Othello: She turned to folly, and she was a whore.
Emilia: Thou dost belie her, and thou art a devil.
Othello: She was false as water.
Emilia: Thou art rash as fire to say
That she was false. Oh, she was heavenly true!
Othello: Cassio did top her. Ask thy husband else.
Oh, I were damned beneath all depth in hell
But that I did proceed upon just grounds
To this extremity. Thy husband knew it all.
Emilia: My husband?
Othello: Thy husband.
Emilia: That she was false to wedlock?
Othello: Ay, with Cassio. Nay, had she been true,
If heaven would make me such another world
Of one entire and perfect chrysolite,
I'd not have sold her for it.

Emilia: My husband?

Othello: Ay, 'twas he that told me on her first.

An honest man he is, and hates the slime

That sticks on filthy deeds.

Emilia: My husband?

Othello: What needs this iterance, woman? I say thy
husband.

Emilia: O mistress, villainy hath made mocks with love!

My husband say she was false?

Othello: He, woman;

I say thy husband. Dost understand the word?

My friend, thy husband, honest, honest Iago.

Emilia: If he say so, may his pernicious soul

Rot half a grain a day! He lies to th'heart.

She was too fond of her most filthy bargain.

Othello: Ha?   [*He draws.*]

Emilia: Do thy worst!

This deed of thine is no more worthy heaven

Than thou wast worthy her.

Othello: Peace, you were best.

Emilia: Thou hast not half that power to do me harm

As I have to be hurt. O gull! O dolt!

As ignorant as dirt! Thou hast done a deed—

I care not for thy sword; I'll make thee known,

Though I lost twenty lives.—Help! Help, ho, help!

The Moor hath killed my mistress! Murder, murder!

                         act 5, scene 2, lines 130–74

Superbly loyal to the murdered Desdemona, Emilia is fearless, standing up to the armed and crazy Moor. The entrance of Montano, Gratiano, and Iago inaugurates the final movement of Othello's deranged existence:

> **Montano:** What is the matter? How now, General?
> **Emilia:** O, are you come, Iago? You have done well,
> That men must lay their murders on your neck.
> **Gratiano:** What is the matter?
> **Emilia:** [*to Iago*] Disprove this villain, if thou be'st a man.
> He says thou told'st him that his wife was false.
> I know thou didst not; thou'rt not such a villain.
> Speak, for my heart is full.
>
> act 5, scene 2, lines 175–82

That Iago should be unknown, even to his own wife, testifies to his amazing development throughout the drama.

> **Iago:** I told him what I thought, and told no more
> Than what he found himself was apt and true.
> **Emilia:** But did you ever tell him she was false?
> **Iago:** I did.
> **Emilia:** You told a lie, an odious, damnèd lie!
> Upon my soul, a lie, a wicked lie.
> She false with Cassio? Did you say with Cassio?
> **Iago:** With Cassio, mistress. Go to, charm your tongue.
> **Emilia:** I will not charm my tongue; I am bound to speak.

My mistress here lies murdered in her bed—

All: Oh, heavens forefend!

Emilia: And your reports have set the murder on.

Othello: Nay, stare not, masters. It is true indeed.

Gratiano: 'Tis a strange truth.

Montano: Oh, monstrous act!

Emilia: Villainy, villainy, villainy!

I think upon't—I think, I smell't!—O villainy!

I thought so then—I'll kill myself for grief—

O! Villainy! Villainy!

Iago: What, are you mad? I charge you get you home.

Emilia: Good gentlemen, let me have leave to speak.

'Tis proper I obey him, but not now.

Perchance, Iago, I will ne'er go home.

Othello: Oh, Oh, Oh!   [*Othello falls on the bed.*]

act 5, scene 2, lines 183–204

The Moor's internal collapse finds an outward gesture as he flings himself down on the bed of his butchery. Emilia, magnificent in her bitter courage, becomes a freely blowing north wind of truth, to the cost of her life:

Emilia: Nay, lay thee down and roar,

For thou hast killed the sweetest innocent

That e'er did lift up eye.

Othello: [*rising*]   Oh, she was foul!

I scarce did know you, uncle. There lies your niece,

Whose breath indeed these hands have newly stopped.

I know this act shows horrible and grim.

Gratiano: Poor Desdemon! I am glad thy father's dead.

Thy match was mortal to him, and pure grief

Shore his old thread in twain. Did he live now,

This sight would make him do a desperate turn,

Yea, curse his better angel from his side,

And fall to reprobance.

act 5, scene 2, lines 205–16

Kinsman to Brabantio, Gratiano is accurate in believing that Desdemona's father, had he lived, would do the desperate deed or turn of reprobance, that is to say damnation through suicide.

Othello: 'Tis pitiful. But yet Iago knows

That she with Cassio hath the act of shame

A thousand times committed. Cassio confessed it;

And she did gratify his amorous works

With that recognizance and pledge of love

Which I first gave her. I saw it in his hand;

It was a handkerchief, an antique token

My father gave my mother.

Emilia: Oh, God! Oh, heavenly God!

Iago: Zounds, hold your peace.

Emilia: 'Twill out, 'twill out! I peace?

No, I will speak as liberal as the north.

Let heaven and men and devils, let them all,

All, all, cry shame against me, yet I'll speak.

Iago: Be wise, and get you home.

Emilia: I will not.   [*Iago threatens Emilia.*]

Gratiano: Fie,

Your sword upon a woman?

Emilia: Oh, thou dull Moor! That handkerchief thou speak'st of

I found by fortune and did give my husband;

For often, with a solemn earnestness,

More than indeed belonged to such a trifle,

He begged of me to steal't.

Iago: Villainous whore!

Emilia: She give it Cassio? No, alas! I found it,

And I did give't my husband.

Iago: Filth, thou liest!

Emilia: By heaven, I do not, I do not, gentlemen.

O murderous coxcomb! What should such a fool

Do with so good a wife?

Othello: Are there no stones in heaven

But what serves for the thunder?—Precious villain!

[*He runs at Iago; Montano disarms Othello.*]

[*Iago, from behind, stabs Emilia.*]

Gratiano: The woman falls! Sure he hath killed his wife.

Emilia: Ay, ay. Oh, lay me by my mistress' side.   [*Exit Iago.*]

act 5, scene 2, lines 217–45

Returned at last to reality, the Moor invokes the stones or thunderbolts of heaven and is prevented from killing Iago by Montano's intervention. Iago, as we would expect, stabs Emilia in the back and escapes momentarily. Exquisitely prolonging our suffering, Shakespeare subjects us to Emilia's repetition of Desdemona's willow song:

Gratiano: He's gone, but his wife's killed.

Montano: 'Tis a notorious villain. Take you this weapon,

Which I have here recovered from the Moor.

Come, guard the door without. Let him not pass,

But kill him rather. I'll after that same villain,

For 'tis a damnèd slave.

Exit [with all but Othello and Emilia, who has been laid by

Desdemona's side].

Othello: I am not valiant neither,

But every puny whipster gets my sword.

But why should honor outlive honesty?

Let it go all.

Emilia: What did thy song bode, lady?

Hark, canst thou hear me? I will play the swan,

And die in music. [*She sings.*] "Willow, willow, willow."

Moor, she was chaste. She loved thee, cruel Moor.

So come my soul to bliss as I speak true.

So speaking as I think, alas, I die.　　　　　[*She dies.*]

act 5, scene 2, lines 245–60

The counterpoint of Othello's self-regarding "Let it go all" and Emilia's "I will play the swan" surpasses what has been called "the *Othello* music." This contrast continues in her proud "So speaking

131

as I think, alas, I die" and the Moor's desperate attempt to reassert
a warrior's dignity:

> **Othello:** I have another weapon in this chamber;
> It was a sword of Spain, the ice-brook's temper—
> O, here it is. [*He finds a sword.*] Uncle, I must come forth.
> **Gratiano:** [*within*] If thou attempt it, it will cost thee dear.
> Thou hast no weapon, and perforce must suffer.
> **Othello:** Look in upon me then and speak with me,
> Or, naked as I am I will assault thee.
> [*Enter Gratiano.*]
> **Gratiano:** What is the matter?
> **Othello:**   Behold, I have a weapon;
> A better never did itself sustain
> Upon a soldier's thigh. I have seen the day
> That, with this little arm, and this good sword,
> I have made my way through more impediments
> Than twenty times your stop. But oh, vain boast!
> Who can control his fate? 'Tis not so now.
> Be not afraid, though you do see me weaponed;
> Here is my journey's end, here is my butt
> And very seamark of my utmost sail.   [*Gratiano steps back.*]
> Do you go back dismayed? 'Tis a lost fear;
> Man but a rush against Othello's breast
> And he retires. Where should Othello go?
>
>   act 5, scene 2, lines 261–80

Something of his old self returns as he realizes the vanity of his boast. He has reached the butt or limit of his arrow's flight, the beacon of his final voyage. Gratiano need not be dismayed, for even a reed would disarm Othello. Something in him breaks with "Where should Othello go?"

[*He turns to Desdemona.*]

Now, how dost thou look now? Oh, ill-starred wench!
Pale as thy smock! When we shall meet at compt,
This look of thine will hurl my soul from heaven,
And fiends will snatch at it. Cold, cold, my girl?
Even like thy chastity. O! cursèd, cursèd slave!
Whip me, ye devils,
From the possession of this heavenly sight!
Blow me about in winds! Roast me in sulphur!
Wash me in steep-down gulfs of liquid fire!
O Desdemon! Dead, Desdemon! Dead! Oh! Oh!

act 5, scene 2, lines 281–90

When he will meet Desdemona at compt or the Day of Judgment, her slain beauty will send him to hell. The enigma of an unconsummated marriage lingers in her cold chastity. The Moor himself is the cursed slave and seeks the fires of hell. The entry of the captive Iago, accompanied by Lodovico, Montano, and poor Cassio, who has to be carried, hastens the final recognition:

Lodovico: Where is this rash and most unfortunate man?

Othello: That's he that was Othello. Here I am.

Lodovico: Where is that viper? Bring the villain forth.

[*Iago is led forward.*]

Othello: I look down towards his feet; but that's a fable.

If that thou be'st a devil, I cannot kill thee.   [*He wounds Iago.*]

Lodovico: Wrench his sword from him.   [*Othello is disarmed.*]

Iago: I bleed, sir, but not killed.

Othello: I am not sorry neither. I'd have thee live,

For in my sense 'tis happiness to die.

Lodovico: O thou Othello, that was once so good,

Fall'n in the practice of a cursèd slave,

What shall be said to thee?

Othello: Why, anything.

An honorable murderer, if you will,

For naught did I in hate, but all in honor.

act 5, scene 2, lines 291–303

Shakespeare does not allow us the illusion that the Moor truly apprehends the sufferings of others. The dramatist's aesthetic dilemma is how can you restore some dignity to this great ruin of a warrior.

Lodovico: This wretch hath part confessed his villainy.

Did you and he consent in Cassio's death?

Othello: Ay.

Cassio: Dear General, I never gave you cause.

Othello: I do believe it, and I ask your pardon.

Will you, I pray, demand that demi-devil
Why he hath thus ensnared my soul and body?
Iago: Demand me nothing. What you know, you know.
From this time forth I never will speak word.

act 5, scene 2, lines 304–12

Those are Iago's last words. He will die mutely under torture.
His prime affect is now outrage, probably provoked by Emilia's
unexpected courage.

Lodovico: What, not to pray?
Gratiano: Torments will ope your lips.
Othello: Well, thou dost best.
Lodovico: Sir, you shall understand what hath befall'n,
Which, as I think, you know not. Here is a letter
Found in the pocket of the slain Roderigo;
And here another. [*He produces letters.*] The one of them
    imports
The death of Cassio, to be undertook
By Roderigo.
Othello: O villain!
Cassio: Most heathenish and most gross!
Lodovico: Now here's another discontented paper
Found in his pocket too. And this, it seems,
Roderigo meant t'have sent this damnèd villain;
But that belike Iago in the interim
Came in and satisfied him.
Othello: [*to Iago*]   O thou pernicious caitiff!

How came you, Cassio, by that handkerchief
That was my wife's?
Cassio: I found it in my chamber;
And he himself confessed it but even now
That there he dropped it for a special purpose
Which wrought to his desire.
Othello: Oh fool, fool, fool!
Cassio: There is besides, in Roderigo's letter
How he upbraids Iago, that he made him
Brave me upon the watch, whereon it came
That I was cast; and even but now he spake,
After long seeming dead, Iago hurt him,
Iago set him on.
Lodovico: [*to Othello*] You must forsake this room and go with
        us.
Your power and your command is taken off,
And Cassio rules in Cyprus. For this slave,
If there be any cunning cruelty
That can torment him much, and hold him long,
It shall be his. You shall close prisoner rest
Till that the nature of your fault be known
To the Venetian state.—Come, bring away.

                              act 5, scene 2, lines 314–47

Presumably Othello faces trial and execution, yet we cannot be
certain. Since he has been the indispensable commander of the
Venetian forces, we may wonder whether they would have pre-

served him as a captive mercenary who might still be of some use. But the Moor chooses his own conclusion:

> **Othello:** Soft you; a word or two before you go.
> I have done the state some service, and they know't.
> No more of that. I pray you, in your letters,
> When you shall these unlucky deeds relate,
> Speak of me as I am; nothing extenuate,
> Nor set down aught in malice. Then must you speak
> Of one that loved not wisely but too well;
> Of one not easily jealous but, being wrought,
> Perplexed in the extreme; of one whose hand,
> Like the base Judean, threw a pearl away
> Richer than all his tribe; of one whose subdued eyes,
> Albeit unusèd to the melting mood,
> Drops tears as fast as the Arabian trees
> Their medicinable gum. Set you down this;
> And say besides that in Aleppo once,
> Where a malignant and a turbaned Turk
> Beat a Venetian and traduced the state,
> I took by th'throat the circumcisèd dog,
> And smote him, thus.   [*He stabs himself.*]
>
>   act 5, scene 2, lines 348–66

T. S. Eliot, seconded by F. R. Leavis, dismissed this dying oration as merely an instance of Othello "cheering himself up." That seems inadequate to the complexity of the suicidal Moor. Indeed, he indulges in a kind of special pleading, yet his yearning for a lost dignity touches us. He weeps as he speaks, and there is still self-deception. He did not love well enough, and was easily jealous. Perplexity remains his key signature, as he still falls short of understanding his flaws. I follow the Folio reading of "Judean," where I read the reference as Herod the Great, who killed his wife Mariamne in a seizure of jealousy.

It is difficult not to feel ambivalence when Othello passes this final judgment upon himself. Whether or not some shred of dignity is restored to him is debatable. And yet his final turn to Desdemona is heartbreaking:

Lodovico: O bloody period!

Gratiano: All that is spoke is marred.

Othello: I kissed thee ere I killed thee. No way but this, Killing myself, to die upon a kiss.   [*He kisses Desdemona and dies.*]

Cassio: This did I fear, but thought he had no weapon; For he was great of heart.

Lodovico: [*to Iago*]   O Spartan dog, More fell than anguish, hunger, or the sea! Look on the tragic loading of this bed. This is thy work. The object poisons sight; Let it be hid. Gratiano, keep the house,   [*The bedcurtains are drawn.*] And seize upon the fortunes of the Moor, For they succeed on you. [*To Cassio*] To you, Lord Governor, Remains the censure of this hellish villain,

The time, the place, the torture. Oh, enforce it!
Myself will straight aboard, and to the state
This heavy act with heavy heart relate.   *Exeunt.*

act 5, scene 2, lines 367–82

Cassio's tribute is just: "For he was great of heart." The genius of Iago proved too strong for Othello's mind to sustain. Lodovico speaks for all of us, who have to sustain "this heavy act with heavy heart."

Despite the apocalyptic intensity of *King Lear* and *Macbeth*, I reread them with exuberant pleasure, since the sublime calls out to our own answering sense of glory. But nothing by Shakespeare makes me suffer as *Othello* does. Iago remains the most dangerous of all villains, because his infernal intelligence throws us into despair.

ABOUT THE AUTHOR

Harold Bloom is Sterling Professor of the Humanities and English at Yale University and a former Charles Eliot Norton Professor at Harvard. His more than forty books include *The Anxiety of Influence*, *The Western Canon*, *Shakespeare: The Invention of the Human*, *The American Religion*, *How to Read and Why*, *Stories and Poems for Extremely Intelligent Children of All Ages*, *The Daemon Knows*, *Falstaff: Give Me Life*, *Cleopatra: I Am Fire and Air*, and *Lear: The Great Image of Authority*. He is a member of the American Academy of Arts and Letters, a MacArthur Fellow, and the recipient of many awards and honorary degrees, including the American Academy's Gold Medal for Belles Lettres and Criticism, the Hans Christian Andersen Award, the Catalonia International Prize, and the Alfonso Reyes International Prize of Mexico.